VOICES OF BRITISH COLUMBIA

Robert Budd

foreword by MARK FORSYTHE

STORIES

from our

FRONTIER

VOICES OF BRITISH COLUMBIA

Douglas & McIntyre
D&M PUBLISHERS INC.
Vancouver/Toronto/Berkeley

Copyright © 2010 by Robert Budd

10 11 12 13 14   5 4 3 2 1

All rights reserved. No part of this book may be reproduced,
stored in a retrieval system or transmitted, in any form or by any means,
without the prior written consent of the publisher or a licence from The Canadian
Copyright Licensing Agency (Access Copyright). For a copyright licence,
visit www.accesscopyright.ca or call toll free to 1-800-893-5777.

Douglas & McIntyre
An imprint of D&M Publishers Inc.
2323 Quebec Street, Suite 201
Vancouver BC Canada V5T 4S7
www.douglas-mcintyre.com

Cataloguing data available from Library and Archives Canada
ISBN 978-1-55365-463-6

Editing by Derek Fairbridge and Lucy Kenward
Cover design by Jessica Sullivan and Peter Cocking
Text design by Peter Cocking and Jessica Sullivan
Cover photographs courtesy of Royal B.C. Museum, B.C. Archives: (clockwise from top left)
HP093186/Hannah Hatherly Maynard, HP003761, HP093991, HP008228
Map by C. Stuart Daniel/Starshell Maps
All interior photos courtesy of Royal B.C. Museum, B.C. Archives
CD compilation edited and produced by Robert Budd
CDs manufactured in Vancouver, B.C., by CDman
Printed and bound in China by C&C Offset Printing Co., Ltd.
Printed on paper that comes from sustainable forests
managed under the Forest Stewardship Council
Distributed in the U.S. by Publishers Group West

We gratefully acknowledge the financial support of the
Canada Council for the Arts, the British Columbia Arts Council,
the Province of British Columbia through the Book Publishing Tax Credit
and the Government of Canada through the Book Publishing
Industry Development Program (BPIDP) for our publishing activities.

To my mother, Vivian,
and in memory of my father, Les Budd (1946–2008)

Contents

FOREWORD *xi*
INTRODUCTION *1*

(1) ORIGINAL VOICES 9

Put Your Knife Down 11
LIZETTE HALL
on the Meeting of James Douglas and Chief Kwah

Won't Do Anyone Any Good to Fight 17
DANNY MILO
on Natives and White Men during the First Gold Rush

(2) TO THE NEW COUNTRY 21

Not Knowing What I Was Coming To 23
ARTHUR SHELFORD'S
Adventures as a Newcomer

Those Mountains Were Our Garden 31
PADDY ACLAND'S
Life as a Remittance Man in the Okanagan Valley

Now You Are My Brother 39
AGNES JOHNSON
on Medical Missionary Robert Tomlinson

To Climb the Rockies 51
EDWARD FEUZ
on Mountaineering in the New World

Oh, Just Some Place To Go 57
IVOR GUEST
and the Journey from Vancouver to South Fort George

(3) THE GROWTH OF NEW CITIES 63

Horse and Buggy Days 65
ROGER MONTEITH
and Victoria in the 1890s

The Town Was Changing So Fast 73
ISABEL SWEENY
on Early Days in Vancouver

(4) WORKING OUT WEST 79

Gold Was Lying on Top of the Ground 81
ARTIE PHAIR
and the Lillooet Gold Rush

I'll Sell It To You Cheap 91
GUS MILLIKEN
and the Hills Bar Claim

There's No Sound…There's Nothing! 95
BILL LACHANCE
the Sole Survivor of the 1910 Glacier Snowslide

Paid by the Skin 105
MAX LOHBRUNNER
on the Seal-hunting Life

(5) PIONEERING WOMEN *115*

Cried Every Day for a Year *117*
MRS. H. WILLIAMS
on Making a New Home

Monarch of All I Survey *125*
SARAH GLASSEY
the First Woman to Pre-empt Land in British Columbia

This Country Was a Dream *135*
MYRA DEBECK
on Her Mother's Rustic Life

(6) A FRONTIER CHILDHOOD *143*

Youngsters Haven't Got Any Fear *145*
NELLIE BAKER
and Wild Horses in the Thompson

No Children Here *151*
WALTER WICKS
on Life as a Child at a Remote Salmon Cannery

**(7) LEGENDARY FIGURES
AND HISTORICAL CHARACTERS** *157*

More Trader Than Missionary *159*
AGNES HARRIS
on Robert Cunningham and the Founding of Port Essington

He Was a Robin Hood *163*
MARTIN STARRET
on the Capture of Bill Miner, the Legendary Train Robber

There's Old Cataline *169*
MARTIN STARRET
on B.C.'s Most Famous Mule Packer

The Hanging Judge *175*
TOM CAROLAN
on Matthew Begbie's Frontier Justice

The Queen of Kitselas *179*
WIGGS O'NEILL
on a Bizarre Bootlegging Trial

BONUS TRACK *185*
Busting Comrades Out of the Clink
ARTHUR SHELFORD
Recounts a Jailbreak

EPILOGUE *187*
AUTHOR'S NOTE
ACKNOWLEDGEMENTS

FOREWORD

It's in the Voice

MARK FORSYTHE

THE HUMAN voice soothes, nurtures, connects people. Recently a new mother was telling me how her baby had been fussing most evenings, so she sang a tune she'd crooned during her pregnancy. As her daughter heard the first notes of Joni Mitchell's *Both Sides Now*, she calmed. Instantly. The human voice is a wondrous and powerful thing; we catch its rhythms, its nuance, its rise and fall, even in the womb.

Imbert Orchard knew the power of the voice. He listened to a thousand voices as he and CBC Radio recording engineer Ian Stephen lugged tape recorders around British Columbia to interview the people who founded this province, including Aboriginal people whose stories reach back thousands of years. Today, those audio archives sound as fresh as the day they were recorded: they're crisp, warm and personal. We hear apprehension, humour, sadness, reflection, and realize the things that make us human are all wrapped up in the sound of our voices. Even a pause during a conversation can be revealing as someone searches for the right words to give their story clarity and meaning (or avoids answering a question we've posed). We hear people think during such moments.

The fact that the Canadian Broadcasting Corporation encouraged these two to travel across B.C. to gather so many stories is commendable, especially since many of these interviews were never aired. CBC recognized the value of building this first-person archive, which is exactly

FACING: *Imbert Orchard interviewed hundreds of British Columbians. This map shows the locales described in the twenty-four stories reproduced here.*

what a public broadcaster should be doing. These memories and stories are our social history and provide context for our times.

In this world of sound bites, long-form interviews like the ones conducted by Imbert Orchard are very rare indeed. Today we don't have the patience to listen, to attempt to understand the broader context of what's behind those sound clips, to sort through the fragments of information charging toward us via radio, TV, cell phones, the Internet. Tuning in to the radio for a one-hour conversation between Imbert Orchard and one of his pioneer subjects would be unheard of today. We're partial to the fragments, even if we don't know what they mean.

Imbert Orchard, though, knew he was on to something when he began talking with B.C.'s pioneers. He was also an excellent listener and guided conversation in a masterful way, much like another great CBC radio interviewer, Peter Gzowski. When he was interviewing, Peter thought of himself as sitting at the back of a canoe, steering, with his guest riding up front. Peter understood the overall direction of the interview and guided that journey by listening carefully then dipping his paddle in the water, asking a question or making a well-placed comment to keep the conversation on course. In Peter's interviews, his guests did almost all of the paddling: the story propelled them toward their destination, often with an enlightening detour or two along the way. In his own way, Imbert Orchard did much the same thing. He sat away from the microphone. Listening carefully, and posing simple, direct questions, he encouraged his guests to tell their story. In their own words.

My CBC colleague Deborah Wilson has spent hours listening to many of Orchard's oral history interviews as she prepared profiles of B.C. characters and events for broadcast. She comments that listening to him interview people in his gentle, unhurried way was to be, "transported to another place and time…What I learned from Imbert Orchard: slow down and savour the details."

Orchard tapped memories like some people tap maple trees. The stories flowed, and the range of experience was remarkable. He asked about places like Port Essington on the Skeena River, a canning community that no longer exists yet is no less a part of the story of British Columbia. He met Joseph Coyle, who moved from New Jersey to Alaska then to

Aldermere, near Smithers, where he launched the area's first newspaper and described how his newsprint was carried into the valley by the legendary packer Cataline. (Coyle went on to invent the egg carton.)

In his collection, we hear first- and second-generation memories of a vast province being opened up by riverboats, railroads and cattle drives. Imbert listened to Annie York of Spuzzum tell him about her grandparents' recollections of Simon Fraser as he descended the river to Lytton during his search for the mouth of what he thought was the Columbia River. And he heard her sing the same Aboriginal songs that would have greeted Fraser. He drew out the stories of homesteaders on Read, Hornby and Theodosia Islands, tales of pioneers who followed Aboriginal grease trails and Alexander Mackenzie's route into the Bella Coola Valley. Orchard teased out details that would otherwise have been lost forever, and in retelling their experiences, the pioneers re-experienced these events like they happened yesterday.

In 1980, my friend Brad Daisley had a summer job cataloguing the Orchard Collection. Two things stood out for him from that experience. "The first was the misconception that oral history is nothing more than 'grandpa's stories.' Listening to Imbert's recordings was like crawling inside history and being part of it. These were living people who cried, laughed, who sighed as they recounted not just the extraordinary events that made British Columbia, but also the mundane occurrences, so often forgotten by historians, that were the foundation for those more important events. Conventional history tells you about building the early roads from Vancouver to New Westminster; Imbert's people make you feel every single wheel rut along the way. And unless you know how much those ruts hurt, you will never know why a new road was built."

The second lesson was the realization that Orchard's work was unique in this relatively young province. "Starting his recording in the 1960s allowed Imbert to capture the voices (the actual sounds) of some of B.C.'s earliest European immigrants and of the Aboriginal people who knew of the first contacts... Add to that the incredible quality of Imbert's recordings and you have one of the best oral history collections in the world." Jean Barman, one of the province's most important historians, has called Orchard's work one of the "two principal sources for getting at the everyday attitudes and actions of everyday people in British Columbia, historically, from their own perspectives." (James Matthews is the other.) The recordings have been a fundamental component of her ongoing research on British Columbian history.

Although I never met Orchard (he was hired by the CBC the year I was born), we do share a few things in common. We're both refugees from Ontario who have been smitten by our adopted province—its landscape, its people and a history you can still reach out and touch. We both became public radio broadcasters because we were drawn to this most personal of electronic media, where connections are made solely through the sound of the human voice. And we have both travelled much of the province to record interviews. I've been fortunate to meet with people like the late Nisga'a leader James Gosnell, who with arms outstretched boomed that his people had lived in the Nass Valley for thousands of years. I've met farmers in the Peace River Valley who worry their land will be swallowed up by the next dam project, and I've met scientists who are tracking orca whale families in Johnstone Strait.

Things have changed at CBC since Orchard's time. We don't interview the pioneers any longer. We don't honour stories from our elders as he did. And we don't send people off to gather interviews that won't necessarily make it to air. To be sure, some of our longer-form documentary work does capture our times in a compelling way, and more CBC Radio and TV archive material is available through our Web services. Thankfully, we also employ people like archivist Colin Preston who sees great value in the treasure that Imbert Orchard left us, but worries it may be the last such archive.

"Those of us who ply the craft of Sound & Moving Image archiving these days are unlikely to have the challenge and pleasure of preserving and creating access to a contemporary collection as rich and complete as Imbert Orchard's. It's a vexing paradox: there is more 'content' in the digital world, yet collections of ideas and memories are more fragmented than ever. The operative term in the production world is 'paralysis by analysis.' We have more 'bits' of information than we can possibly deal with, but all too often we lack the 'frame' to place the content within a coherent whole. We can 'aggregate' material from all sorts of sources, but what of its provenance, its context?

"That this seminal Orchard Collection was preserved and catalogued so well is a wonderful confluence of happy accident, Orchard's own diligence and the professionalism of the B.C. Provincial Archives."

It's easy to ignore the past. In a province where many people come from elsewhere, it's no wonder we're missing that sense of where we've come from, and how it informs where we may be going. In this sense, Rob "Lucky" Budd's efforts to re-ignite interest in these stories is encouraging and exciting. Just like a field that grows vigorously after lying fallow, the stories in Orchard's collection may generate new interest in the province's history and its pioneers. Listen to the enclosed CDs of Orchard's interviews and resist the urge to regard these voices as quaint and distant. Try to imagine yourself in their time—inside their dreams and struggles. They're not so different from our own, and they may have lessons for us yet.

INTRODUCTION

Imbert Orchard and the Story of the Province

"I'm surprised how few people know about our great characters and the people who are semi-historical, semi-legendary that are in B.C. We've got just as rich a background as any part of this continent in that way, but we don't know it yet."
IMBERT ORCHARD, in an interview with J.J. McColl, June 1973

WHEN THE Canadian Broadcasting Corporation (CBC) hired Imbert Orchard in its Vancouver office in 1955, little did the broadcasting company realize what a legacy he would leave. As a regional editor he was responsible for receiving and reading television scripts, but it was a chance encounter with Constance Cox, an elderly Native woman from Hazelton, that changed his future. The day she walked into his office and declared, "The other day I saw a program about the [Klondike] Trail of '98; I was there!" then proceeded to tell Orchard how the CBC had got the story all wrong, he had no idea that his decision to write her biography would be the genesis of one of the largest oral history collections in the world. Still, he borrowed a tape recorder from his secretary and began to record Cox's story.

The interview tapes sat around for a few months until Orchard and CBC producer John Edwards got talking one day, and the two men came up with the idea to do a fifteen-minute radio series about the Skeena River based on Cox's experiences and the accounts of a few other people

FACING: *Imbert Orchard, CBC radio producer and oral historian, on a field-recording trip in northern B.C., 1971.*
Photo: I-67699

Orchard knew in Vancouver. As he became fascinated with the idea of recording more stories from the Skeena River area, he and sound technician Ian Stephen travelled from Prince George to Prince Rupert by boat, "picking out the people who were worthwhile as far as broadcasting was concerned."

As Orchard explained to interviewer J.J. McColl in 1973: "Once you get into a community, it's very easy to get from one person to another. Most people who have lived there a number of years will know who the old-timers are, who are the characters who can tell the story from way back. Well, you go and visit these people and you find that one's memory isn't half as good as other people think it is... but then you find the really good people who have marvellous recall and are still quite bright, and they feel like talking to you... I'm very interested in the fact that this way of doing things, going through the country in that way, you find the story of the country; you get them to tell you the story of the country and the story of their experiences in the country. So I'm not looking for any particular subject, as a rule."

Born Robert Henslow Graham Orchard in Brockville, Ontario, in 1909, Orchard had first come to British Columbia as a member of the Canadian Armed Forces during the Second World War. He fell in love with the province right away and set about learning as much about the history of the place as he could. He went to a local library and was surprised that he could find very little information about his new home, and that what he did find was somewhat anecdotal. Years later, in February 1978, he told Derek Reimer at the Provincial Archives of British Columbia: "And that fired me, you know; with a little bit of the background of B.C., immediately I got interested. I could see this was another story altogether, and a richer one than what I was used to in Ontario.

"I feel that Ontario is very rich... the development that took [place at] that time in Ontario—from 1790 to 1970, if you like—that period is 'squeezed up' in B.C. In about a hundred years less of time, it's come from the bush to the big cities. This is a fantastic development. This country interests me because of that.

"It also interests me because of the stories, as I got to see them, were rather large scale; they were kind of 'epic'... the Indian presence was much stronger here. It was a much more challenging life, therefore it produced a different kind of person. And also, I realized that there was a tremendous variety in this country. There is more variety in climate and terrain between Long Beach and the Rockies than there is in all the rest of Canada... I began to see that this was a story all by itself and almost a country all by itself."

To uncover this "story," and inspired by his experience on the Skeena River, Orchard travelled over 24,000 miles by boat, horse, car, train and foot and interviewed nearly a thousand people between 1959 and 1966. He used a fraction of the material in three series, *Living Memory, From the Mountains to the Sea* and *People in Landscape,* which he produced and broadcast on CBC Radio in the 1960s and '70s. In 1974, when the Provincial Archives of British Columbia established an aural history program, Orchard donated approximately twelve hundred tape recordings (all of the original master tapes of the interviews, as well as the original master tapes from the completed episodes from each of the three radio series) to the Archives, where they are still housed today. In all, the Orchard Oral History Collection (not including the finished radio programs) amounts to 998 interviews (in excess of 2,700 hours) with miners, ranchers, fur traders, ship captains, missionaries, farmers, totem carvers, road builders and some of the First Nations people of British Columbia.

Orchard was already fifty years old when he began to collect his interviews, and as he was not doing the job to make a name for himself, the interviews remained largely unknown. He, himself, was struck by how little British Columbians knew about their own heritage:

. . .

ORCHARD: Yes I'm surprised how few people know about our great characters and the people that are semi-historical, semi-legendary that there are in B.C. We've got just as rich a background as any part of this continent, in that way. But we don't know it yet.

You see, I realized early on that it was no good waiting for a special occasion or a special budget, that I was going to have to go out and get a lot of these people before they died. Luckily again, the CBC cooperated with this idea, and Ian [sound technician] and I travelled all over the

CD I, TRACK I

country just to get the people, before they died or before they faded out. And this was what I did. And then it's there to be used, but I haven't had the opportunity to use a great deal of it.

Of course this gave me a sense, too, that what I was collecting was not just for the CBC. I was collecting it for the province, for the story of the province, for an understanding of the life of those days. And to me that was ample justification for getting all this stuff that wouldn't get on the air for some time.

And of course the important thing now is to gather this up and have a means of preserving it, because we don't know how long tape will last. I know some tape disintegrates after twelve or fifteen years, very rapidly. Now we've got to have a means of preserving this tape so that fifty or a hundred years from now these voices can still be heard. They're part of our story, the story of our country. And it's very, very important to do that. I discovered this early, early on, I knew that the tapes I was doing were going to, if I could preserve them, would play a part, a certain historical part, a certain part in preserving the history.

We need facilities for research. Not just simply research for the historian, the academic person who's only concerned really with writing—but for people who want to go back to the original and listen, and hear how it sounded and how this person's meanings come through in sound, which they don't come through on the written page. You've got to go back to the original thing if you're going to get the meaning of it.

And telling a story, and this is very, very ancient and it's way beyond before print was ever invented. And it's coming back into its own now. And this is to me very important.

. . .

ONE of the intentions of this book, then, is to expose British Columbians to the valuable resource Orchard has left us and, by including the original audio recordings, to realize his vision.

Although the B.C. Archives have been instrumental in preserving Orchard's work, his contribution to oral history and the Orchard Collection itself remain largely unknown by scholars and the general public. In the 1970s to early 1980s, the B.C. Archives published a series of books

An audiotape copying setup used by the B.C. Archives' aural history program, 1975. Photo: I-67663/Janet Cauthers

entitled *Sound Heritage* that used excerpts from the Orchard Collection along with material from other collections. In the 1980s, the Sound and Moving Images Division (SMID) at the Archives created a catalogue system for the Orchard Collection. However, it was not until the summer of 2000, when the CBC embarked on a project to digitize all of the audio material scattered across the country in the various provincial archives, that his material came to light again. Under the supervision of Allen Specht, the long-time director of SMID, Charlene Gregg and I were hired to begin cataloguing and copying to compact disc all of the reel-to-reel tape and other recordings that belonged to the CBC and were housed at the B.C. Archives in Victoria. In 2001, we began to work on the Orchard Collection.

In the course of digitizing and cataloguing this enormous and extensive collection, I sat with headphones on for hours, listening to the interviewees tell their tales. Often I was taken back to another time through the tremendous sense of atmosphere conveyed in the voices and stories of the collection. Less than a week into listening, I came across a couple of tapes titled *Patenaude—Horsefly*, which were recordings made of my very good friend Pharis's great-grandfather and great-grand-uncle. The Patenaudes were one of the first non-Native families to settle in the Cariboo region (Pharis is the fifth generation to come from Horsefly), and it struck me then that the tapes I was accessing contained stories about people's great-great-grandparents discussing familiar places and speaking in English. (My own relatives would have been speaking Central European languages!) It became clear to me that each of these accounts was a window into the history of this province that no one else had ever heard in its entirety.

The more I listened, the more I felt that I had to help get this material out so the general public could have access to this rich resource. As a result, the Orchard Collection became the focus of my master's degree in history at the University of Victoria. Contained in this book, several years later, are the "greatest hits" from the collection, a broad survey featuring fun, poignant stories from a variety of regions and covering an array of vocations and experiences that paint a picture of life in pre-war B.C.

Since the contents of this book are a sample of the entire collection, there are many omissions. For example, I have not selected any of the stories from northern Vancouver Island or from the Arrow Lakes district. And the collection itself contains many interviews from the Skeena River but very few from the Stikine River. These omissions are not meant to take away from the rich histories in each of these areas, but I could not represent everything in this one volume.

It is also worth noting an obvious oversight in Orchard's collection: Asians—particularly Japanese and Chinese people—are discussed in many interviews, yet among all the recordings in the collection there is only one interview with a Chinese person. Perhaps Orchard did not deem the level of their English or the quality of Asian immigrants' voices to be "broadcast worthy." Perhaps they refused his requests to be interviewed or perhaps he didn't think to ask them. Regardless, much information can be gathered from Orchard's collection about how the Chinese and Japanese people of British Columbia were perceived by non-Asians in the pre-war period. Workers of Chinese origin were segregated in British Columbia's labour markets: mostly they competed with Euro-Canadians for low-wage manual-labour jobs, though some Chinese and Japanese people were also independent proprietors—mainly farmers and fishermen. Orchard's informants, some of whom worked alongside Asian labourers, were acutely aware of the Asian presence in the workforce and their attitudes toward Asians were both positive and negative, reflecting many racial assumptions and some tension in society at large.

Similarly, Orchard had tremendous respect for Aboriginal oral tradition and believed the cultural stories passed down from generation to generation were the property of the nations from which they came. As a result, he did not focus on these stories. Most of Orchard's interviews with Native peoples fall within the realm of oral history, which is to say their personal recollections about what everyday life was actually like as British Columbia went from a settlement with a hundred or so non-Native people in January 1858, before two gold rushes and Confederation, to almost 400,000 by 1911. As conveyed in the Orchard Collection and in this book, the province's past is the story of newcomers settling the frontier in western Canada; it is a story of people accommodating to and building infrastructure in B.C.'s vast landscape in the nineteenth and first part of the twentieth century.

Voices of British Columbia, the book and the accompanying audio recordings, are intended to immerse you in the history of British Columbia: read the introduction to each story, listen to the speakers narrate their own experiences while you follow along in the text and look at the various photos and map. Discover a sense of place and meet the personalities who shaped the province, including Orchard himself who speaks with and prompts his interviewees. Through these audio recordings, Orchard has provided a window into the remembered past, allowing British Columbia's pioneers to speak for themselves. As he said to Derek Reimer in 1978: "My contribution was to get people to see that... the sound of a person's voice is an historical thing in itself. And the feeling that's in that voice, as voice, not what comes on the page afterwards, is historically important." I am hopeful that these samples from the collection, both audio and visual, will encourage you to look for details about B.C. history in general or even about your own specific family histories amid the material at the B.C. Archives or your local archives.

(1)

Original Voices

BRITISH COLUMBIA'S First Nations are steeped in a rich oral tradition that communicates much about their diverse cultures and about the history they created before Europeans came to this land. Although these stories—the legends and traditional narratives—are the property of the individual nations from which they come, they are a fascinating and invaluable part of the province's historical record. However, to respect the sacred nature of these stories when talking to Aboriginals, Imbert Orchard focussed on people's individual memories rather than on their broader cultural reminiscences.

In the following two stories, Native speakers discuss the interaction between Native and non-Native people at and before the first gold rush of 1858, which brought the largest wave of immigration to British Columbia.

FACING: *Aboriginal people near Lytton, ca. 1870.*
Photo: HP000676/Frederick Dally

Put Your Knife Down

LIZETTE HALL

on the Meeting of James Douglas and Chief Kwah

(RECORDED SEPTEMBER 19, 1966)

LIZETTE THERESE HALL was a member of the Dakelh (Carrier) First Nation, an indigenous people who are part of the Athapaskan language group that occupies a huge area from the upper Fraser River up to Anahim Lake in the Chilcoten region and that also has a strong presence in the Nechako River area. Hall's father was Chief Louis Billy Prince, born in 1864. Hall's great-grandfather was Chief Kwah, born in 1755, who was chief of what is now the Nak'azdli Indian Band.

Hall's story begins with a discussion of first contact between the first Europeans and the Native people in her area, in 1806. Chief Kwah lived near Fort St. James and was instrumental in preventing Simon Fraser's men from starving when they were camped at Stuart Lake. A natural leader, Chief Kwah saw to it that the thirty to forty thousand salmon needed to feed Fraser's men annually were secured. As one of the traders commented in Jean Barman's book *The West beyond the West*, Kwah "is the only Indian who can and will give fish, and on whom we must depend in great measure. It behooves us to endeavour to keep friends with him." Chief Kwah was greatly respected by both the Native and non-Native communities at the time of the following anecdote about Sir James Douglas in 1828.

Often credited as "The Father of British Columbia," Sir James Douglas (1803–1877) was a British colonial governor at the time and was of

FACING: *When this photo was taken in 1896, Bob, a Yu-Ka-guse medicine man, was 104 years old. He was one of the few elders who remembered seeing Simon Fraser in 1808.*
Photo: HP016181/W.H. Barraclough

central importance during this phase of the province's history. Schooled in Britain, he had come to Canada at the age of sixteen to enter the fur trade for the North West Company, an outfit that eventually merged with the Hudson's Bay Company (HBC). In 1828 he married Amelia Connelly, daughter of William Connelly, the Chief Factor of the fur-trading district of New Caledonia, and a Cree woman (Hall mentions that Douglas's wife is "a half-breed"). In 1840, Douglas became Chief Factor of the HBC, the highest possible rank for field service in the company, then in 1851 he became the second Governor of Vancouver Island. The following anecdote involves Douglas while he was a clerk at Fort St. James on Stuart Lake, working for the Hudson's Bay Company.

. . .

CD1, TRACK 2

HALL: Well, my father was, he was the chief, until his retirement in the '40s, I think, he retired. They had hereditary chiefs, you know, in the old days and he was born in 1864, according to the register.

ORCHARD: Are there any memories handed down of the first white men coming, and what was the impression of them?

HALL: Yes, the people were living up here at Sowchea. They had, there was a reserve still there yet. But that's where they were living in the summertime when these saw these canoes around the point and they were singing, the canoeists were singing. And they saw these canoes and they all went on the shore to see who it was. They were singing in a strange language, something they hadn't heard before. So they were all there when they landed, and they were white men. I guess that would be Simon Fraser—when they first came.

And they all crowded on the shore to see. They were very curious, of course. They hadn't seen any white men before and they started, I suppose, they talked in sign language. They couldn't understand one another, you know.

And they showed them different things that they had, you know, like a knife and soap. They didn't start to eat, according to all these stories that you hear, that they started to eat the soap. My father said they didn't start to eat the soap. He said they didn't know—they didn't give them any soap in the first place to begin with, but they showed them a knife and then they showed them a— they showed them a gun and they fired the gun. When they fired the gun, well, they all took for the bush, you know. They got scared. They had never heard anything like it. They did all their hunting by these homemade things like spears, and, well, they did their hunting by spears and snares and traps, these wooden traps.

The first two came from McLeod's Lake. They arrived where the Hudson Bay is. Yes, there were two white men. Yes, two years before he [Simon Fraser] came. No, a year before he came. They arrived where the Hudson Bay is. Not exactly where the store is—that's the fourth store, the Hudson Bay, you know. Anyway, they arrived. It was just overgrown with great big spruce, and so they came out there and one of them made a blaze on the tree and said, "This is where the post will be." And he promised the people that in a year's time they would come back and build a post, where they could buy knives and guns, you know, and various things.

Sir James Douglas, 1860s. Photo: HP002653

There was a trail from McLeod's Lake, yes, ninety miles [145 kilometres] because there was a post above McLeod's Lake before Fort St. James. They didn't call it Fort St. James in those days. It was called Stuart Lake, Stuart Lake Post.

ORCHARD: Any incidents from those earlier years?

HALL: There was a, I guess everybody knows about how James Douglas's life was threatened.

ORCHARD: That was here, was it?

HALL: Yes, that was here.

In the 1890s, an aboriginal smokehouse was a gathering place as well as a location where fish, including halibut, were hung to dry. Photo: PN00366

ORCHARD: What was the story about that?

HALL: Well, apparently this Native [named Zulth-Nolly] gave a beating to some Hudson Bay servant down in Fort George and, according to the story, he killed him and then he sneaked back up here. It was during the summertime, during the salmon season, and all the people were camped at the mouth, close to the mouth of the Stuart River.

And this man came up and, of course, he was hiding, and as soon as they heard about it across the lake there at the post, a couple of the men, the Hudson Bay men, came over and starting searching for him. Didn't know, they saw them coming, you know, but there was a woman who had a baby and she was in bed, of course that would be in the smokehouse. And he didn't know where to hide, so finally they hid him. He crawled in with this woman. He didn't know at the last moment, he didn't know where to go, so he just jumped there and, well, these two men, they came searching. And, of course, they threw the blankets off this woman like they did in the old days, like the Hudson Bay used to do, you know. They bossed these Natives, and so they threw the blankets off her, and there the poor fellow was crouching. And they got him out and they just tore him, literally tore him to pieces, and killed him.

Kwah was away then. He was down the river at that time. And they tore this poor fellow, just tore him to pieces without any fair trial, without even asking any questions. They just yanked him outside the door and they just literally tore him to pieces outside.

And when Kwah came back he was furious, of course. He was down the river at that time, and when he returned and found out what happened, well, he, Kwah, had a terrible temper and he took his men across. He said, "We will go and avenge this man's death. They had no business to come over when I wasn't here to do such a thing to one of my people."

So he went across with some men. He picked these men, and they went across to the fort and they were let in. The fort was inside a barricade, a stockade, they call it. So when they got there, he demanded to see James Douglas who was a clerk then. And, or was he a clerk?

Anyway, he was there, and he, so they all got in the fort, right inside the trading post and demanded to see. One of the men had a knife and he went and grabbed James Douglas. Well, James Douglas started to order them out, you know, and no, they weren't going to budge.

They said, "We're staying right here. You had no business to come to our camp and do what you did to this fellow, and upsetting the whole village," because all the children got scared and the women were just, the children were all screaming, you know, running around there while they were searching for this man.

Well, I guess James Douglas was, he really started to tell them off. And one of the fellows grabbed him by the throat, and he said he held him like that with a knife upraised in his right hand, and he said to Kwah, "Shall I strike?"

And Kwah didn't say anything. So, "No," he said. "Don't strike, yet," he said. And this fellow at the throat of James Douglas was just, you know, he really wanted to kill him right there, and finally Kwah said, "No!" He said, "Let him go."

So this woman, I guess it would be James Douglas's wife who was upstairs. She was a half-breed and she came down, and according to

"He once had in his hands the life of (future Sir) James Douglas, but was great enough to refrain from taking it," reads Chief Kwah's gravestone. Photo: HP071315

my father she didn't throw anything down. According to the stories, is that she threw blankets and clothes down there and to pacify the men, but she didn't. I asked my father, you know. It was just between my father and I, and I know my dad wouldn't lie to me.

I said, "Is it true?" I said, "that this woman threw down blankets and dresses and stuff like that to pacify?"

He said, "No, she just came down and said—she was crying, of course, and she said, 'Please don't kill my husband. Please, I'm one of you, too, and he's my husband and I love him. Please don't kill him.'"

So he said, "Put your knife down," he said to the fellow, "and let him go." So the fellow let him go and didn't kill him.

There's a lot of things that are written that are not true about the Native people and their ways like they say. Like, my tribe, they're the Carrier, and they say that they used to carry the bones of their husbands on their backs. According to my father, that isn't true. They didn't carry them, the bones, on their back at all. He said he had never heard of this. I told him what was written, and he said "I never heard of such a thing." He said they used to bury them in the trees, sort of cache them, I guess. And they would bury them later, I guess. After the white man came, they showed them how to bury their dead.

But the story about James Douglas, well, it's been retold so many times, and a thing added here and a thing added there. Well, this is the true story of what, just what did happen.

ORCHARD: How did they resolve that problem?

HALL: Well, they talked about it after he told the fellow to—this man—he let him go. And he didn't want to let him go, but Kwah said to let him go, so he had to take his hands off James Douglas. And then they talked about it, you know, and so they left quite peaceably after that. Well, remember that there was no law, no policemen or anything, and these Natives were used to protecting one another and protecting their wives and their families.

Won't Do Anyone Any Good to Fight

DANNY MILO

on Natives and White Men during the First Gold Rush

(RECORDED IN APRIL 1963)

DANIEL MILO (1864–1966) was 98 years old at the time of this interview. Born in Sardis, B.C., in the Fraser Valley as a member of the Chilliwack First Nation, Milo outlived all eleven of his brothers and sisters. His parents lived in a home on the banks of the Old Chilliwack River, and when he was a child, the current swelled and the family home was washed away. He offered many flood stories to Orchard. Milo also illustrates a lot of history and some oral tradition about the Chilliwack people, including details about geography, particularly that of Cultus and Sumas lakes.

Here, Milo discusses details about what is now known as the Fraser Canyon War, which took place in the fall of 1858. The combatants of the war were six impromptu regiments of immigrant gold workers from around Yale, and the Nlaka'pamux (known in English as the Thompson or Hakamaugh). The centre of Nlaka'pamux territory was called Camchin, the modern-day townsite of Lytton. Gold panning in the area greatly disrupted the riverbeds and, consequently, the livelihoods of many First Nation communities. The tensions escalated when the Nlaka'pamux retaliated for the rape of one of their young women by French miners and sent decapitated bodies downriver. Many miners panicked when bodies began to circle in the eddies by Yale, the centre of commerce.

There were two regiments of particular importance: 1) the Whatcom Company was formed of mostly southern Americans and was led by

Captain Graham. They were enthusiastic about a war of extermination as a means of dealing with anything that stood in the way of their search for gold, and 2) New York's Pike Guards were the most influential of all the regiments and were led by Captain Snyder. Snyder had correspondence with Governor James Douglas in Victoria and sought a peaceful resolution to the conflict. Snyder urged the members of all regiments to make a distinction between "friendly Indians" and "hostile Indians."

The townsite of Lytton, 1875. Photo: HP037815

All but two or three men in the Whatcom Company died in a nighttime gun-battle, but there were no Aboriginals involved. A panicked reaction to a rifle falling and discharging had led the soldiers to shoot one another. Meanwhile, the Nlaka'pamux war leader wanted to exterminate the non-Natives, but as Milo describes, the Chief Cxpentlum (known as David Spintlum in English), who had a good relationship with Douglas, managed to broker a peaceful pact with Captain Snyder. Six treaties were made after the meeting, though none of them exist in any form to this day.

Milo discusses two groups of "Indians" in his anecdote: the Chilliwack and the Nlaka'pamux, or Thompson, Nations.

. . .

CD1, TRACK 3

MILO: You know, the Indians, when I first hear them speaking about the white man. In them days, those white people, they were travelling on the way to the gold rush. They were starving. Because they were starving, they had nothing to eat on the way through. Well the Indians began to feed them, feed them until they get all right, and then they start again.

They say the Indians here in this valley, Chilliwack Valley, are about the kindest Indians that's living. That's what the white people said.

They got way up at the canyon. On that time, there was no road at all, just little trails for the Indians to travel on. Well those Indians got mean, and they drowned a lot of them that were walking through that trail. My father used to tell me, every once and while, he'd see a man drifting with a pack, drifting down the river. Well, they found out what was going on up there, wherever they send the armies from, around Victoria, I guess, or New Westminster. They sent them up to stop them people, or kill them, because they kill a lot of white people going up to the gold mine.

They come there, these armies, and look around the place there. They don't see any man that is fit to be going around at all. Just old people, women, that's all they see.

And there was a man that was living at Lytton. He was the head man of all that speaking. Thompson language, you see. There was a man, the head of that speaking, you see. He lives at Lytton. His name was Spintlum. He come down there and see the army was right there, ready to catch any Indian that's around there.

He started to talk to them. "I don't think it will do anybody any good at all to go and fight about this. I'll talk to them myself."

"Those men are down some, you can't find them. Them people, they know the whole place of these hills here, mountains. They go up there, you can't get them."

"So it's just the good way for you people to just let it go, and I'll talk to them to quit that." That's what this Spintlum said.

Well, the army said, "All right. We wish that you would do that, and talk to them not to do it anymore." So they quit. They started to build a road then from Yale to the gold mine. They began to have pack horses, wagons.

When I was a boy, I see a pile of wagons there at Yale, what they use going up to the mines, see, and pack horses, you know. It was the Spanish people using the pack horses, you know. They're the ones that understand how to use pack horses.

(2)

To the New Country

In the thirty years between 1881 and 1911, the non-Native population of British Columbia swelled from 23,798 (6,514 of whom were actually born in British Columbia) to 372,306 (64,316 of whom were born in the province). The Orchard Collection sheds light on the experiences of many of these new immigrants, and the stories in this chapter reveal how they adapted to a new culture, a burgeoning economy and an often inhospitable landscape. Such a small population spread across such a huge area invariably led to lots of local "grass-roots" political movements.

Anyone coming to the West had to want a rustic lifestyle, as a lot of work had to be done to learn to live in such diverse terrain. The province's varied landscapes—from mountains to prairies to deserts to coastlines to alpine tundra—gave rise to many diverse stories and ways of life. However, all immigrants to British Columbia shared a sense of adventure and a drive to adapt, to not be defeated.

FACING: *A freight team passing 150 Mile House.*
Photo: SW1805/Frank Cyril Swannell

Not Knowing What I Was Coming To

ARTHUR SHELFORD'S
Adventures as a Newcomer
(RECORDED NOVEMBER 9, 1961)

ARTHUR SHELFORD (1885–1979) imparts a very detailed story about coming to Canada from England, learning several skills while working various jobs and navigating a massive area until he found the lifestyle that suited him. Shelford was one of many thousands of people who immigrated from England in the first decade of the 1900s. Though his story is unique, it shares many elements typical of others' experiences at the time.

Shelford arrived in Canada in 1908, in the midst of a dramatic economic depression. He mentions the 1907 collapse of the Knickerbocker Trust Company, which was one of the largest banks in the United States and served as a trust for both individuals and corporations. In 1907, the Trust was caught using its funds to drive up the cost of copper by cornering the market, and the National Bank of Commerce, one of the larger banks at the time, declared that it would no longer accept money from the Knickerbocker Trust. Panic ensued as the stock market plummeted, and having lost confidence in the banks, many people withdrew their money. The result was that all of the people who depended on the Trust were left destitute, and many banks went bankrupt.

Although it was centred in the United States, the depression was felt in Canada and Europe as well. Thus, when Shelford came to Canada, employers had a tremendous amount of power over a desperate labour force. As he describes corruption and exploitation in the labour force and

FACING: *The steamship* Inlander *entering Kitselas Canyon, 1911. Photo: HP029366* details about wages, Shelford's account evokes the atmosphere of life in British Columbia during this depression.

Shelford's story centres around two areas of British Columbia. The first is the small town of Field, which lies within Yoho National Park, twenty-seven kilometres west of Lake Louise, in the Rocky Mountains on the Alberta/British Columbia border. Field was established during the building of the Canadian Pacific Railway (CPR) as a locomotive depot for pusher engines to help trains over the nearby mountain passes. There, Shelford worked on an "extra gang," a crew that works outside maintaining the railroads. After working his way across the province, Shelford, with his brother Jack, staked some land in the Ootsa Lake district of northern British Columbia, long occupied by the Wet'suwet'en First Nation and located at what is now the northern tip of Tweedsmuir Provincial Park. It was a 240-kilometre round-trip journey to the nearest store and twice that to the nearest doctor in Hazelton, and Shelford describes the trials of finding their land and building on it.

. . .

CD1, TRACK 4

SHELFORD: My early life in England had been very quiet and very peaceful and happy. I'd been at school. I was 19 in just a small country village in North Hampshire and I went in the civil service but I couldn't see any future in it. And when I looked at the old men in the offices and saw what they came to, I just couldn't see myself living there until my life end.

The older men, when I talked about coming to Canada, they thought I was very foolish: giving up a good job, not knowing what I was coming to in Canada...

"Haven't got a job?" they said. "Darn fool, going to Canada. Doesn't know what he's going to do even!"

But there was one man in that office which I shall always remember, Pat McKay. He was an older man.

He came to me and he says, "Shelford, don't you take any notice of these people. You go out there. Don't you stop in this office all your life. I have," and he said, "I know what it means."

So I jumped my job. I came to Canada with the untold thousands that were coming to Canada at that time. The *Virginian*, on which I came, was just loaded to the gunwales with enthusiastic emigrants that were just the same as myself—didn't know what they were coming to. They just came. I don't know what it was. It was just an urge and that's all there was to it.

And when you came to Canada in those days, you just had to do anything. You couldn't pick your jobs. When I came, in 1908, there was not even a minor but a fairly big depression on. The Knickerbocker Trust in the fall of 1907 had gone broke and that had started quite a serious depression. And even when I left London, there was all kinds of marches by the unemployed there. And it was very much the same when I came to Canada.

And so when I got to Calgary, there I was a victim of a very common practice. The bosses of a job and the employment agents, working together, especially in a big job like the tunnel work at Field, and at a time when there were very few jobs going, they worked in cahoots. The boss fired the men, employment agent hired them and they shared the dollar. In fact, it got so bad later on that the provincial government had to stop the private employment agents and do all the employing work by the provincial agents.

At last I thought I'd better get a job of some sort, so I went to another employment agent and went to get a job on a section. So I went on the extra gang at a dollar and a half a day. And at a dollar and a half a day, I was getting more than I was getting in the British Civil Service after passing, being at school until I was 19 and passing a highly competitive examination, which didn't look too bad. And, in those days, at a dollar and a half a day, you could even save a little money.

You paid four and a quarter for board and the rest was yours, and we worked a lot of overtime. I had a very good time on that extra gang. There was one car of, we will call "white people," and the other car was mostly Eastern Europeans—quite nice fellows.

I had it knocked out of me pretty quickly that the British were the only nation in the world, that the other people from the others were just as good when you got used to them, mingled with them, worked with them. Bright happy fellows, good workmen and good neighbours, we'll call them. I spent about six weeks on there.

We had a good foreman, a big fine Norwegian, Jack Norman. And the finest boatman I'd ever seen, cheeriest, good boss! He made you work though. You didn't get by without that. The first day I worked I got there at noon. I worked until two o'clock that morning, shovelling gravel onto a flat car.

I may mention one thing that I learned at Field, and that was that without gloves you got some pretty bad blisters on your hands. And I was really glad to get fired at Field because my hands were a mass of blisters and I couldn't have kept on working if they hadn't fired me.

Now, I had gloves. No trouble with my hands at all. It was my back that suffered this time.

Spring of 1909, I felt like getting a move on and then I got into Vancouver—all the trees coming out nicely in bloom and the leaf and the flowers in bloom—everything was just beautiful! Vancouver, in those days, wasn't as big as it is now but it was quite a sizeable town and a very nice place to be.

There was one thing that impressed me was, though, most people seemed busy buying and selling real estate. They'd buy it from one fellow one day and sell it to another fellow, or back to the same fellow perhaps, the next day. It was just a real game. I think most of them lost their shirt when the First World War came on. They couldn't pay the taxes on the land they'd bought, a good many of them. But otherwise, they enjoyed themselves anyway. But I was never a gambler, hadn't got much money anyway to invest in real estate, and so I never bought any.

When my brother [Jack Shelford] came up later, to see me, he had been to England, from Alaska, and he came to suggest that we went up to northern British Columbia to look for land. Well, again, I jumped my job. I don't quite know why, but I suppose the urge to get land was in my blood. So we went down to Vancouver and got a bit of an outfit, went up to Rupert, up that beautiful Inside Passage and, from Rupert, we travelled up the Skeena by riverboat.

Well, we came up the Skeena. It was a lovely trip. The steamers were the old rear-paddlewheel and fired by wood, which they got from wood camps at the side. When we got to Kitselas, we had to disembark and cross overland by wagon with our goods. We walked over, of course, to the other side of the Kitselas Canyon.

In middle water, that can be navigated by the steamers; but, in low water or high water (and it was really high when we came up), the steamers just couldn't get through there. Below the canyon, it was quite nice travelling, all by Terrace and all up to Kitselas. After Kitselas, it was pretty rough going. A big sidestream caught our bows and swished us around, and we looked as though we were going to wipe our nose on a big bluff there.

Jack got pretty startled, and I was more than startled. But we got by. We had to inch our way up sometimes in the swift current. The crew had to go out in a boat and take a line up to a deadman [a beam of wood], and we had to winch ourselves up beside using our paddlewheels. But all in all it was a very nice trip. As always, in those kinds of trips, you got interesting company. People from everywhere, people with families coming up from California—I remember one of them—others from other parts of the States. I remember a German American.

But, at last, we got up to Hazelton. Hazelton was just a little frontier village but full of life because there were all men from the camps along the Grand Trunk Pacific, which was in construction. I guess the bars were always full of the Omineca, and the Ingenico Hotel, and pack trains were going out to all different places, and wagons were going out loaded with supplies. Altogether it was a very busy place from our point of view.

But, of course, we had to get on. We had decided to find land in the Interior. I don't know; the Ootsa Lake country seemed to beckon to us and so we decided to go there. We had to get a pack horse to take our blankets and our grub. We had to walk.

And so we went down the valley, a lovely trip down that valley: lovely poplar timber and big open spaces, lovely vegetation, except in the mornings. It wasn't so lovely then when you went to hunt your horse. It was waist high and just dripping with dew, and you really got wet if you hadn't got waterproof leggings, which we fortunately had. All the road in, you met different people, just the same as yourself—searching for land, wondering what they should do in life, trying to find a place to settle down in.

It was very interesting because they came from all parts of the globe, all parts of US, Canada, European countries, everywhere.

Eventually, we got to Houston. It wasn't Houston in those days, it was just a store there run by Herb Silverthorn. Then, we had to go into the Ootsa Lake country—just a trail. You didn't meet many people there because there weren't many people coming in and out of that country. It was a little off the general line of travel, but there was a trail. We got there.

When we got to Nadina, we had to swim the horses. There was no bridge there, but we got across.

Well, we wandered about in that country. It's a country of numerous lakes, hundreds of them. It's called the Lakes District. There were lakes and creeks, plenty of fish in them, plenty of grouse. It was out of season, of course, but nothing's out of season to a hungry man. And I'm afraid we transgressed the game laws a little sometimes and we ate some grouse sometimes. Quite a nice diet, too. It was very interesting walking along. You didn't seem to mind the walking. You'd got to go and find something. That was all there was to it, and you walked until you found it.

Looking for land wasn't an easy matter in those days. There were no survey lines of any kind in the country at that time. All you'd got to go on was if you happened to see a stake stuck up in the brush, mostly a poplar tree cut off and squared at the top with a notice on saying that somebody was intending on applying for that land.

It was rather remarkable how you did happen on most of those stakes. I suppose it was that the stakes were put in the land that looked good to the people. Went and climbed the hills and looked to see if there was any land because a lot of it was timber, the Jack pine and spruce type.

The land mostly, the good land, was poplar timber and that's what we had to look for. We climbed Picket Hill, as we called it, west of our place now, looked over there. There was no land down there. And we got near to our place and we climbed another big hill and we saw a beaver meadow, a big beaver meadow, two big beaver meadows for that matter. We found our way to them, and there was home.

And then we had to go out to Hazelton, a hundred and fifty miles again, walk out. We'd already walked, I suppose, must have been well over two hundred miles [320 kilometres] with all our wanderings, must have been two hundred and fifty [400]. We had to walk another hundred and fifty [240] to get out to Hazelton to record our land at the land office. And we did so.

Then we had to get an outfit. We had to winter in there. Fortunately, Jack knew something about an outfit. I didn't. We got two other horses, Romeo and Billy, two fine little pack horses. Billy was a little old but he served us very well. But Romeo was just a little dear—no other word described him. I'm sure if there'd been a Juliet, she'd have fallen in love with him.

You couldn't resist Romeo anything he wanted. If he wanted salt or sugar you just had to give it to him, and as a pack horse he was perfect. He could pack all those small eight pack, three hundred pounds [136 kilograms] without flinching all day unless you had a ruffled blanket. If you'd

A fully loaded packhorse, 1912.
Photo: HP008780/W.W. Wrathall

got a ruffled blanket, Romeo just went into the brush and said, "I'm not going any farther until you fix this blanket." And he wouldn't do anything. He would stand there. You couldn't make him travel, but you fixed his blanket and Romeo was a good pack horse again.

So we got our outfit. We had to buy a winter's grub. What grub? Some of you fussy people might not like our diet. It was just flour with some baking powder, bacon, beans, rice, dried apples and tea, sugar and rolled oats. And we had some cornmeal to vary our morning diet from the rolled oats, and that's all we had. And we enjoyed it! We were hungry! We were young! That was good grub and we ate it.

George Turner and Bill Adams whip-sawing lumber.
Photo: HP007387

But we couldn't pack all our outfit in. We'd got nails and traps and we'd got one weapon, the whipsaw that we had to buy. We'd got to get some lumber when we got in there. There was no sawmill within, at that time, within at least a hundred miles [160 kilometres] of the place and so there was no road to get lumber in if you bought it. And so we'd got to whipsaw it.

We'd got quite a load to bring in, so we had to hire an Indian, Tom Campbell, to take about half a dozen horses. I forget whether it was half a dozen or ten horses he had, to take our load to Houston, what we couldn't carry on our three horses. He it was who taught us how to pack an *appareil*, to keep the pack on it.

We got to Houston, and there we took over for ourselves. We had to relay. I think we had five relays into our country to get our outfit in. Then came the job of building the cabin. We had to have somewhere to live.

In the meantime, we were living in the tent. We built the cabin but we made one mistake: we put a roof on, a dirt roof. A dirt roof is all right in dry weather, but a dirt roof in wet weather is a mean contraption. It just rains through and drips for days after the rain stops. That's the trouble.

We were too eager to get on with other work that we hadn't got the sense to take a little time, cut a few shingles or even hollow out some scoops, as they're called, put anything on to keep that rain from coming through. And we suffered five years of misery in wet weather living in that cabin, just because we hadn't the common sense to put on a decent roof until we got our cabin fixed. We had to whipsaw all the lumber for the floor. We had to whipsaw all the lumber for the window, and Jack made the window. We'd got a little glass in with us, and he made the window himself because he was a good carpenter. He'd been an apprentice carpenter in the old country and was a good one.

Those Mountains Were Our Garden

PADDY ACLAND'S
Life as a Remittance Man in the Okanagan Valley

(RECORDED NOVEMBER 12, 1964)

HENRY VIVIAN "Paddy" Acland (1883–1968) served with the British Army in the Second Boer War (1899–1902, in what is now South Africa) before his father suggested that he move to British Columbia in 1908 as an alternative to army life.

Starting in the 1880s, many British men emigrated to Canada but received a regular remittance (or allowance) from their families. As a result, they came to be known as remittance men. In most cases, these men were paid by their families to stay away because they tended to cause problems or embarrass the family. As British tradition held that first-born sons were entitled to family inheritances so that the family wealth would remain in one place, most remittance men were second sons and often regarded as a financial drain on the family. Acland may not have fit this stereotype, but it is clear that Acland's father was concerned as to how his son was to earn a living.

Once Acland arrived in British Columbia, he learned to build log houses. After that he worked for a tobacco farmer in Kelowna, as a government weed inspector and on a dairy farm. Later still, he sorted lumber and surveyed, among other jobs. Not all remittance men were as industrious as Acland, however; the Orchard Collection contains many stories of remittance men who drank their allowances away or found other colourful ways of squandering their money.

ABOVE: *Raspberry canes, ca. 1900s. Apparently Paddy Acland's acreage wasn't suited for this kind of farming.* Photo: HP037075

Here Acland describes his experience coming to the arid, sunny Okanagan Valley. Non-Native ranchers began to settle around Okanagan Lake in the 1860s, and commercial apple orchards were first cultivated in 1892. Acland settled near the community of Summerland in 1908. Originally founded in 1848, the settlement on the western shore of Okanagan Lake was incorporated as a municipality in 1906 by the president of the Canadian Pacific Railway, Sir Thomas Shaughnessy, and John Moore Robinson who enticed future orchardists by claiming that Summerland had "summer weather forever!"

In this anecdote, Acland provides a glimpse of the lifestyle of remittance men living in B.C., and it illuminates elements of the political process in the Okanagan Valley at that time.

. . .

ACLAND: I've often thought about this in my latter part of my life. Why a lot of fellows weren't killed out here, I don't know. They did the most damned stupid things but they always came through all right. There was very seldom a man killed. There was my young brother just out of school, seventeen, and myself—I had been a soldier, it's quite true—and another fellow that had never been out here, and we used to walk about those mountains just as if they were our garden. We'd go back the whole day and never think of anything. We'd always come back.

But years later, when I'd settled down there, I was always surprised. I'd get fellows who'd been brought up in this country, and during the hunting season they'd come to my place and throw the door open and throw themselves flat on their face and slap the floor with their hands and say, "I'm lost! I'm lost!"

I said, "How the hell can you be lost? You're here. I've found you!"

"Well, I know but I don't know where I am!"

I said, "You're with me. You're all right. Now get up and have some supper."

But this used to happen about twice in every hunting season. I think that the answer to it is this: that a lot of us young fellows came out here. We got to know the Indians. We liked the Indians. I certainly did. And I knew more about finding my way around the country from just

CD1, TRACK 5

TO THE NEW COUNTRY 33

conversations like I'm having with you with an old Indian than anybody could tell me who lived in a city or a town.

And he said to me when I was going out hunting the first time, frankly, he said, "Now look here! Where you're going, this is damn rough country. Always look behind you. Before you go into a place, look behind you and find something you can see for a long way and then go on again and keep doing that and you'll always find your way out!" And I think there's a lot of truth in it.

Now, another trick that the Indians do and white men don't do—and I think it's a pity some of them don't—is they don't blaze, just walking into the woods. They take little branches and they snap them off, and as long as they can see the last one they snapped off, they go straight on and when they come back they come straight back, following these branches. I've watched them do it.

It's interesting, particularly because I'm just one out of a hundred of them just the same. Directly after the Boer War, there was not only a lot of unemployment but the Liberal government decided to cut the army down. I came out for this reason. My father sent for me and he was a soldier and he said, "You haven't got a chance of getting on. You'd better get out!"

When I was having this interview with my father, he was all hopped up about a place—he didn't know where it was—called the Okanagan Valley. Well, he had a cousin who was going to make a fortune out of these orchards. It was just as simple as that to him, that you came out here and you bought a ten-acre orchard and you made a thousand a year out of it—pounds. If you bought twenty acres [eight hectares], you made two thousand a year. That sounded all right.

An Okanagan log house, ca. 1900s. Photo: HP046336

So he asked me what I thought of it. Well, I never thought about the two thousand a year or the thousand a year. The moment I was—talked about British Columbia, my idea was riding horses and hunting grizzly bear and everything else, you know, that sort of business. And becoming as wild as possible, which suited me fine. I was just one that felt the same way.

We hadn't the foggiest notion what we were coming out to. I came out with a sort of young armoury and two or three rifles and shotguns and things to make cartridges with and a tent, and I had everything in my mind.

ORCHARD: In those days, I suppose you did very much what your father told you to do. Or he arranged things for you.

ACLAND: Well, yes. Well, I think we all did in England, you know, more or less. Of course, Father held the purse strings in the first place and he had good reason to hold them tight from me because I could sure get rid of money in a hurry. And when I came out here, I came out with damn little. I was no question a remittance man and I remember, to show you— and I was only one of many—the very first thing I did here was to buy a horse. I practically spent every penny I had buying a horse, though I'd been here a week. I brought my own saddles and everything but I came out in 1908 and I was born in 1883. So I must have been, what was that, about 24, wasn't I?

When I arrived at Summerland—now, Summerland was just one side of a street practically, and there was a little hotel and there, in that paper you got there, a little store and there was a Summerland Development Company.

And they were opening up the upper part into orchards then. And J.M. Robinson had bought a tremendous lot of land there for about a dollar an acre and he was subdividing it, and I went out to work and I put my tent up on the flat, as it was known then, and there were no houses in view at all. And there I lived and I got a job, pick-and-shovel work, working for the Summerland Development Company.

And I picketed my horses out on the flat there, which is now a town. And I was joined by another fellow who was just about as green as I was, and we used to ride about with imitation lariats and so forth. In fact, the horses were the cause of both of us getting sacked from the Summerland Development Company because we were continually losing the horses and not going to work. We had to go and look for them.

I must tell you, at this period, I went back and bought this place that I—which was a pre-emption. I gave somebody a hundred dollars. It wasn't worth fifty cents. But I liked it. It was a pretty place.

And I bought it. And I went out to settle there and I hadn't the foggiest notion what I was going to do out there. But finally, I went and I built my first log house. And I would never have known how to build my log house if it hadn't been that I'd worked for this old fellow, Johnson.

And one day, he told me to get up there at half past five in the morning and we pulled out for another pre-emption, and we—that day, we cut the logs and put them up and put up a lean-to roof on it and roofed it over. And the only thing we hadn't done was to cut out the windows and the doors. You know how you build a log house? You put the walls up and when you come to where you're going to have a door you just put a saw cut in, you see. And you finish the house, then you cut out the door and you cut out the windows the same way. And that's how I learnt to build a log house and that's how I learnt to build that log house that I showed you the picture of just now.

When I wrote to my father and told him I had now got a hundred and sixty acres [sixty-five hectares] and I'd pre-empted another hundred acres [forty hectares] beside me, well, he said, "I got a paper from the British Columbia government in which they state a case near you—that is, in Vernon—where a man is making four hundred dollars off a quarter acre of raspberries, and with your forty or fifty acres cleared already now, you ought to, next year, to be making a considerable amount of money."

So I wrote back and I said, "My dear father, it would cost me more than you'll ever give me to clear that land up. It will cost at least a hundred dollars an acre and even if I had it all covered in raspberries, they wouldn't grow because I'm up too high. And secondly, I'm eighteen miles [twenty-nine miles] from anybody and to bring in even half a ton of raspberries on a wagon over the road that I travel, they would be jam long before I got halfway. So I think you'd better think of something else."

I said, "My only way I can make money out here is to grow something that will walk out for itself, and that's beef or horses." And I said, "There's not much money in either at the present time, I can assure you. I have to go and work out to make a living."

Now, I went home after the—at the end of 1909. I went home for the winter. And I came back and I had a little money then, and I was going to build my house up there. I was a bachelor and I had another bachelor with me, and my brother. And we thought that there was a way up to this place from Peachland. So we stopped at Peachland a night in the hotel then, which was the nearest thing to a menagerie in those days that I've ever seen. There was every creeping thing in it you could imagine, and we stayed the night, and that evening when we got off the boat we ordered about a $120 worth of grub and food and things we needed, and we told the storekeeper to get a big Democrat [wagon] and we'd take it up to my place that was up above on the hills, you see. And it was only about four or five miles [six or eight kilometres] from there, according to the crow flight.

Well, in the morning they told me that they couldn't do it, that it had to go all the way down to Summerland and then back. Back meant that it'd have to go back up this place called Meadow Valley, which was the only way I could get into the place.

So I said, "Well, I'm not going to pay for a buggy to go all the way down there. That's forty-five miles [seventy-two kilometres] odd. I'll have to cancel the order and I'll go down by boat."

And I went down to Summerland, and there I did exactly the same thing but I moved out from Summerland—didn't cost anything like as much. Well, it so happened that this fellow that owned this store was the brother-in-law of the road superintendent, and he went to the road superintendent and he raised all hell because there was no road up to these fellows that were full of money. They were bloody plutocrats going in there to do god knows what and look at the business of this.

Well, eighteen months after the, two years after the—I got a job with some eight or nine other young fellows to build a road down to Peachland, and that road still exists now. But that's the way politics ran in those days.

Now You Are My Brother

AGNES JOHNSON

on Medical Missionary Robert Tomlinson

(RECORDED JULY 12, 1961)

AGNES KATHLEEN JOHNSON'S (b. 1919) grandfather was Robert Tomlinson (1842–1913), an Irish missionary for the Church of England. He came to British Columbia to work as a medical missionary in 1867.

The most prestigious and famous of all missionaries in British Columbia at that time was Anglican lay minister William Duncan (1832–1918), who in 1862 had founded a "utopian Christian community" called Metlakatla, on the Skeena River near Prince Rupert. Tsimshian people from a variety of communities came to live at Metlakatla and were spared from a smallpox epidemic that wiped out nearby communities, something that Duncan told his followers was a sign of God's provenance. In truth, Duncan formed Metlakatla because he believed that in order for the Natives to convert successfully to Christianity, they needed to leave behind many of their traditional ways. However, by 1881 the population of Metlakatla had reached more than eleven hundred, and the Church of England expelled Duncan because of his dissident beliefs and practices. Undeterred, Duncan took eight hundred Tsimshian people to his New Metlakatla in Alaska in 1887.

Robert Tomlinson shared many of Duncan's ideals, and the minister was a huge influence on him. Tomlinson's first duty in British Columbia was to relocate a Nisga'a community from Greenville (now Laxgalts'ap) to Kincolith (now Gingolx) at the mouth of the Nass River. The new settlement became a successful mission in the model of Metlakatla. After

FACING: *Mrs. Tomlinson, née Alice Woods, ca. 1870.*
Photo: *HP007366*

his time on the Nass, Tomlinson decided not to live with Duncan at New Metlakatla, preferring instead to help move the Gitksan people from the town of Kitwanga to a new Christian village named Minskinish (aka Cedarvale). That community, too, was based on Duncan's Metlakatla model.

In the following anecdote, Johnson relates an experience from Tomlinson's time on the Nass River.

. . .

CD1, TRACK 6

JOHNSON: When my grandfather was young, there were seven boys in the family and, of course, as his father, being an Anglican minister in a Catholic country, they were pretty hard up. And the mother, my grandfather's mother, had tuberculosis. And, of course, they didn't know too much about it in those days. And my grandfather said he was going to study medicine so he could learn to find out what caused it and how to cure it.

He made good marks and he got jobs tutoring other students so that he would get enough money to put himself through his medical college. And all the time he did it with the idea that he was going to go through to learn to be a doctor to find out how to beat TB.

Well then, when he was an intern, this call came through, the Church Missionary Society. And, of course, his father, as a minister, received a notification. They were looking for a doctor to come up here.

Mr. Duncan had been here ten years, and the people were dying from TB. Of course, in those days, they didn't know nearly what they know now. But he knew what any other doctor knew in those days: rest and eggs and so on, would be the best they could get anyway. And he came up here then, but he never finished, never waited for his MD. He came up here to do what he could to help the people.

And when he went up the Nass River, one of the first trips he made up the Nass River, he stopped at a village and they brought him a boy that was dying with TB. And he told them that he could do nothing for him because he was dying. He said that—and he explained how the lungs were like bags, and that the TB had eaten holes in the lungs and that he wouldn't live very long.

Then he went on up the river and did some preaching and other work and came back down the river. And when he came back to the village that he had passed through, one of the Christian Natives came out to meet him and told him, "Don't go into the village, because," he said, "if you do, they will kill you because they think that you made the sickness."

And he said, "Why?"

"Because you knew all about it."

Well, he said, "I am going anyway."

So he went and this fellow told him, "They are going to have a feast. They're going to invite you to the feast, and at the feast they're going to kill you."

So he went down to the place where they were preparing the feast, and they had bear skins hanging around the walls, bear skins to sit on, on the floor. And they had kind of a stupid boy, a teenager, but rather stupid, tending the fire while they were waiting for everything to cook, before the women came in to serve it up.

So he says to this boy, "Oh," he said, "What's this?"

The boy said, "That's a bear skin."

He said, "What's a bear?"

So the boy started to tell him all about what a bear was and how it hibernated and what it ate and so on.

And the old man (well he wasn't old then, he was young then), he said, "Well," he said, "You must have made the bear."

"Oh, no, I never made the bear," he said.

"Well," he said, "How do you know?"

"My father told me. My uncle told me. My grandfather told me, all about the bear. Now I'm big, I saw for myself."

And he kept arguing with this boy that he made the bear. Finally, the head men came in and they all backed the boy up. We never made the bear. They all knew about the bear.

Then he turned around and told them how his people had told him about the sickness, and he wanted to know more and he went to school and learned more about it and he had come there to try and help them, but told them, when it got too bad he couldn't do anything. But he was going to try and help them to beat the sickness.

And the head chief took a knife out of his blanket and handed it to him by the handle, and he said, "I was going to kill you." He said, "Now you're my brother."

AND, WHILE he was on the Nass River, he went back to Victoria and married Alice Woods, who was daughter of the first sheriff down in Victoria. After they had spent some years on the Nass River, they came from Ianich, across the grease trail to Kispiox.

Well, Mr. Duncan's policy was to take the Indians out of their own villages and start Christian missions away from the "heathen" influence. And Mr. Tomlinson carried on with Mr. Duncan's policy, so when he went to Kispiox, instead of starting in Kispiox village, he started a new village at Tomlinson's Flats, that's just east of Kispiox village.

After Mr. Duncan broke with the church, the church officials asked Mr. Tomlinson if he would break his friendship with Mr. Duncan or if he would get out of the service. They didn't want him if he wanted to stay friends with Mr. Duncan.

Now Mr. Duncan's main reason for breaking with the church was he did not believe in the use of the surplice or the use of the prayer book. The prayer book, of course, was no use for people who couldn't read, and the surplice was too much like their witchcraft doctors because they were ordinary human beings as long as they were dressed as the others. When they put on their other stuff, their regalia, then they became superhuman.

And he was afraid that the Natives would think, by putting on the surplice, he became superhuman. And he wanted to teach them that they could communicate directly with God, that they did not have to go through some superhuman being. And Mr. Tomlinson followed his line of reasoning, and he said he would rather stay with Mr. Duncan, as he thought Mr. Duncan was correct, than to stay with the church, if he had to choose. He said he would like to stay with the church and remain a friend of Mr. Duncan's, but as he couldn't do both he would keep his friend and let the church go.

And he had planned to leave this part of the country. He went down to help Mr. Duncan to start up New Metlakatla in Alaska, but the people here asked him if he would come back as there was no other doctor in this area. He wasn't really an MD but he had had his medical college and he had taken his internship and was nearly finished when he felt the call to the mission field.

And feeling that an MD—out in the bush—was unnecessary, he came to do what he could for the people who had no doctor of any kind. So he came back and he talked to the people up in this part of the country and said, if he could find a suitable location and the people were willing to go with him, he would go, but they would have to work because there would be no money coming in from the Church Missionary Society—that everyone would have to work and there would be nothing, no help. Before that, part of his salary had gone to help establish the villages, but after that there would be nothing coming in. And so, the people said they would see what they could do.

Robert Tomlinson, medical missionary, 1870s.
Photo: HP041743

All the land belonged to the Indians, and according to their counsel was let out to different people in different traplines. Well, this place at Minskinish belonged to a man named Chief Hep at Kitwanga, and he belonged to the Frog Tribe, or the Kanatas as they called them. And he said he would donate the lower part of his trapline, which is the valley here, including the island, for a Christian mission if they wished to start up.

Well, the people said that would be a good place, and as there across the river, there was a good stream with a waterfall where they could set up a sawmill, they decided to stay to take this place.

So Mr. Tomlinson went back to Metlakatla and arranged to bring his family up to spend the winter of 1887, and that spring, the early part of 1888, with Mr. Price at Kitwanga.

An elderly William Duncan with Native wards at Old Metlakatla, ca. 1910.
Photo: HP002205/John Dean

Now Mr. Price was an Anglican missionary under the Church Missionary Society, but he was a good friend of Mr. Tomlinson's. So the whole family were to move up to Kitwanga for the winter.

On the way up from the coast, they brought several freight canoes with the last supplies that would come up in the fall, and Mrs. Tomlinson and the children—that was Alice who was 15; Lilly, 11; Richard, 9 (that was my dad); Annie, 7; and Nellie, 4—travelled in one canoe with three Indians poling the canoe up the river.

The others had five or six men in to pole, you know, to keep poling and lining, and so on. And Robert travelled with the men, as he was then almost 20, oh I guess about 18. Anyway, he was old enough to go as a man.

Well every day they travelled, and they had an appointed place to stop for dinner. The freight canoes stopped and made a camp and then the others would arrive. They would eat. The family, with the children, would put out the fire and they would leave. The freight canoes went ahead so they had camp ready in the evening, when the others arrived.

The last day, the boys, the Native boys, wanted to get through to Kitwanga to their families; they'd been away a long time. So Mr. Tomlinson said he would leave three older men with the family and they could travel slower and they could stop at Sedan Creek, which is about four miles this side of Kitwanga. And they wouldn't stop for dinner that day, and then the freight canoes could push on and get through to Kitwanga before night.

Well, when they got to Sedan Creek, they had eaten a cold lunch, of course; they stopped here at Minskinish for a few minutes for the children to get out and run around a little, just stretch their legs a little, and went on. And my dad says it was an October afternoon and he said it was very overcast and by four o'clock it started to snow. You know that heavy wet snow that comes down?

Well when you're travelling in a canoe, you have to sit still, especially if you're small, because the captain takes the paddle and hits you over the side of the head if you don't sit still. So they travelled up and they got to Sedan Creek. It was almost dark. They were soaking wet from the snow that had been pelting on top of them, and they had leather boots. In those days there were no rubber shoes up here. I don't know if they had them other places, but they had no rubber boots. They either wore moccasins or leather shoes.

Well, when they got out from under the canvases and covers on the— that were covering their knees and feet, and got out on the shore, the top of them was wet already from the snow. The boys from the canoe gathered up the dry sticks and birchbark, and so on. Mrs. Tomlinson pulled out a piece of paper she had kept in her coat.

She said, "Here's something to start the fire quick."

And they took the paper over, and the captain of the canoe held out his hand and asked her for matches. Of course, she spoke the Native language. They all spoke the Native language when they were with the Natives.

And she said, "Oh, haven't you got the matches?"

"No," he said. "I haven't got the matches. I thought you had the matches."

"No," she said.

So then they started going through all the camping equipment and all the food, and they hadn't one single match with them. Of course, before the white people came, they carried their fire in a container, with them—their coals. But after the white people came with the matches, they relied on the matches, and of course, even in civilization matches weren't too well known in those days. They were rather cherished. Not like they are now.

So they had no matches, and it was getting cold. My dad said my grandmother walked them up and down the beach, and up and down the beach, and the little one, little Nellie, started to cry. And one of the men took her in his arms and took her shoes and stockings off and shoved her right inside his clothes where her cold feet could be up against his body to keep her warm.

My dad said as soon as they realized they had no matches they sent the youngest of the men to Kitwanga. Which would be four miles, and four miles back through the bush, in the snow, in the dark, with no flashlight (they weren't known of), to try and get some matches to make a fire because they couldn't travel. It was too dark. The ice was forming on the edge of the river.

So he said that his feet began to feel numb and his hands began to feel numb and his mother told him, "Keep on moving, keep on walking." And they, they got tired of walking, so she made them pile wood. And he said they had the biggest pile of wood they ever had for a fire. And then the boy came back. Over an hour before he should have got back.

He had met a hunting party that was coming down out of the hills and got some matches from them. My dad said they were all very thankful to see that fire. He said they got their clothes hung up around the fire and crawled into the blankets and they really felt very warm. He said he made up his mind at that time that never would he travel without matches. And he never did, although he was only nine at that time. He always carried matches.

That winter they spent at Kitwanga. Early in March, the next spring, that was 1888, they came down here to Minskinish. The Tomlinson family, consisting of the father and mother and six children, eight Native men and three hand sleighs full of household goods and clothing. That's all the belongings that they had when they came in here, outside of a shovel and a pick and a hoe and a few things of that sort.

When they got here they made up a house just like the Indian houses. The old Indians, before the white men came, used to build their shelters where the cedar trees were growing. They would select trees of about ten inches [twenty-five centimetres] in diameter and cut them off for posts—the outside ones lower than the middle ones. Then they would take smaller cedar trees and put them across the top of the posts, and then use split, hand-split cedar planking, that was split out with the old crude axes that they had, and put it lengthways, that is from the eve of the roof to the ridge pole, leaving a space of about two feet [sixty centimetres] in the centre for the smoke to get out. And then they would put a fire all down the centre of the building, which served for cooking and heating.

Then eight Natives slept on the one side of the fire, and the eight Tomlinsons slept on the other side of the fire. And that was the first shelter here.

They had brought seeds and potato seed with them. And all these, this garden was planted in between the big stumps because they didn't have time to get the big stumps out. Then when they had the garden planted, of course the first month they were there it took them to clean out the rubbish and junk and they planted the garden in April.

They started in and built their cabins. And by fall, there was a log cabin for each family. That was eight families, plus the Tomlinson's was nine, and the log church. Ten buildings the first year, with nine men and some children working. Which I think was very good. As time went on, of course when they got the cabins built, all the men's wives and families moved in.

Then they made a system of how the village was going to be governed. The same system as Mr. Duncan had used in his, following the Indian system of appointing a council among the chiefs who would control the village. And Mr. Tomlinson acted in an advisory capacity. His idea, main idea, and Mr. Duncan's, was to remove the people from the temptation rather than try to remove the temptation from the people.

Mr. Duncan also believed, and Mr. Tomlinson with him, that the adults should be educated as they were illiterate. The Gitksan, Tsimshian and Nisga'a languages are not written languages, although some people have made out a phonetic system for writing those languages, which has worked very well. But, they thought the best system would be to teach them to read and write in English as far as possible, at least to read and write their own names and the names of some places around.

Anyone who could say the alphabet and count to one hundred was admitted to school, whether they were five years old or fifty years old. Then for the church services, they had, on Wednesday nights, they had a prayer meeting. And one other night during the week they had what they called a singing meeting, when they learned a hymn. And at these singing meetings they would take a hymn, for instance like "Jesus, Lover of My Soul." Mr. Tomlinson would read it one verse and explain it to them in their own language. Then they would memorize it in English. They did very well if they memorized one verse in English at one session. And of course they learned the tune. But the Natives are very musical, and rhythm comes very easy to them, so that the singing part was very easy. The English words, of course, was much more difficult.

THEY HAD to have a sawmill because you cannot build lumber houses without a sawmill, and there were no commercial sawmills in the country. Now, Mr. Tomlinson had no money. And Mr. Tomlinson wrote to his friends and relatives in Ireland who were fairly well to do. And they collected amongst others, and collected up enough money for the bare essentials of a sawmill, which wasn't too much. And all the, the pulleys, you know the round ones, were made—handmade out of wood. And the carrier for the lumber was made of wood. They started out with wooden tracks, but they found the wooden tracks wouldn't work because when it got damp they swelled, and the carrier would go crooked, so they had to put in steel tracks. So actually they had to buy the belting and the saw and some levers that couldn't be made out of wood that wouldn't hold.

Kitwanga, 1910. Photo: HP015497

And as soon as they were able to get this equipment up the river, that is the metal part, they set it up on Mill Creek across the river.

In the mean time, Mr. Tomlinson had taught some of his Natives to do very good work with a hand lathe, which he had. One especially was Edward Stewart. And he was the one that carved most of the wood for this, for these pulleys. And that was all the wooden part of the mill was being set up while they were waiting for the other part to come in. So it, I'm not sure if it was the second year or the third year before they got the mill set up.

And when they first came they had no horse. They had no cows either when they first came here, because all that property belonged to the Church Missionary Society. So they had to haul the logs. And they came down off of the hill on the other side of the river, to the mill, with these large logs. The men had ropes over their shoulders, and five or six men would pull the logs so you could tell what kind of logs they hauled down.

To Climb the Rockies

EDWARD FEUZ

on Mountaineering in the New World

(RECORDED NOVEMBER 8, 1964)

EDWARD FEUZ, JR. (1884–1981) achieved notability in the Rocky Mountains because of his expertise as a mountain guide. In this interview, Feuz describes how he came to Canada from Switzerland to be a guide for the Canadian Pacific Railway (CPR) in 1903.

In the first decade of the century, several people had died trying to hike in the Rocky Mountains. The Canadian Pacific Railway owned a number of hotels in the Rockies, and to entice tourists they offered safe guided mountain hikes led by the best mountain guides in the world: Swiss guides from Interlaken, who had had a tradition of hiking in the Alps for centuries. In 1899, Feuz's father, Edward Feuz, Sr., became the first person hired by the CPR from Switzerland. Eventually all three of his sons (Edward Jr., Ernest and Walter) joined him and lived their lives as guides in the Rockies.

Edward Feuz, Jr. settled at Glacier House, which is located in Glacier National Park—just inside the British Columbia border with Alberta. Before Feuz stopped guiding in 1953, completing a fifty-year career, he had led more than 102 new climbing routes and was never involved in any fatalities. He continued to spend time in the mountains after he retired, last climbing 11,365-foot Mt. Victoria (near Lake Louise, on the British Columbia and Alberta border) when he was 85 years old. Feuz Peak, which is the west summit of Mt. Dawson in Glacier National Park, is named for him.

FACING: *A Swiss guide—possibly even Edward Feuz—on the Illecillewaet Glacier, ca. 1900s.*
Photo: HP093571/J. Howard A. Chapman

Here, Feuz recounts an adventure in the mountains with American media baron William Randolph Hearst. Overlord of an empire of newspapers, film studios, magazines, news services and radio stations, Hearst was known for practising "yellow journalism": downplaying legitimate news in favour of enthusiastic and sensational headlines to sell more newspapers. Feuz, however, describes Hearst as a nice man who kept adventurous company.

. . .

CD1, TRACK 7

FEUZ: That's why we were brought out here in this country—to teach the people how to climb the mountains. They didn't know the first thing about it. They walked far too fast instead of going slow, step by step, early in the morning. When you climb the morning. They started to race. They had one or two quite bad accidents. That's why the Swiss guides were a company, the CPR company. They had those mountain hotels: Banff and Lake Louise and Glacier House and Field.

ORCHARD: Could you tell us about how they got in touch with—how did they find, decide to ask your father to come out?

FEUZ: In 1899, you see, that was in Interlaken, Switzerland, and there was an English gentleman named Clark living in town. He was real English. He couldn't speak Swiss. So this news came. He called up my father: he was the chief guide at Interlaken, had all the guides under him, you see. So he called up my father. He had a letter from London, England, from the CPR company, you see. So that started the whole thing, you see. Then my dad went to Canada. I was home. I was the oldest in the family. So when I got on to 15, 16, I went out climbing. All these big things, you see, with people.

And when I got, when was it now, 17 or 18 years? I left school when I got 16, and I got out when I was 17. Then I got, "You can't be a guide," you see, "until you get of age." I got the porter's licence, you know. A porter means you can go along with a party but you must carry the rucksack with stuff in it. There's lots of guides over there, they won't carry only a few pounds, you see, and they had to hire a porter to carry the rope and the provisions and all these things. Therefore, they gave you a licence, a porter's licence.

So, Dad came home, and I'd done all kinds of climbing, you see, and he saw in the papers my name in there, you know, that they got out here in Canada.

So when he come home that fall he says, "I got to see and take you with me to Canada there. You're doing some great things here. I'd like to have you with me."

So he made arrangements with the company, and they accepted me. I was 19 years old and I was here as a porter. And I came out in 1903.

Well, we were all there, so a telegram came down from Glacier that she couldn't accept all the guides. There was a lady manageress there named Mrs. Young. We had to wait there because they were building a new wing on there, a new wing on to the hotel. They hadn't the room, and the guides—they had little guides' quarters there specially built for guides, a little house. And there wasn't the room there. There was workers in the room. They didn't have the room, you see, at the old Glacier house. And, course, I didn't get the pay what the others got paid for, you know. I only had half the pay. So, I stayed there with all the other guides, you know. They used to go, and then lots of times there were two guides to one party, you see, and I went along and was there.

A sleeping porter working for the Canadian Pacific Railway, September 3, 1904. Illustration: PDP07822

I stayed two winters there to learn the language. You know, I couldn't speak any English. I could say "bread" and "butter" and things like that, but I couldn't speak any English. So I stayed there two long winters, I put in there. They were horrible winters up there. So much snow, and the

Cathedral Mountain dwarfing the settlement of Field. The CPR's Mount Stephen Hotel is in the foreground. Photo: I-67927/Melvin McKay Stephens

only live thing we had here was the train, two trains a day, one from the east and one from the west, and they would stop a half an hour to eat.

In those days, they had no dining cars, you know, through the mountains, had no diners. So they stopped there to eat, and then I helped the lady in the office, you know, get the mail in and carry the provisions in. I was a kind of porter there in the winter. And meet all the trains, you know. Sometimes people were tired of trains, from riding in the train, and they stopped over one night. They would stop over, and I carried the baggage up to the rooms, you know.

So after the two winters, I went home, and at 21 and I made the exams. I got my papers. I got my book and then I come out here, again, and I was paid full.

WHEN I was at Glacier, in I think it was '05 and '06, this Mr. Hearst, newspaper-Hearst in California, you know. He came there with a bunch of girls always, young girls, office girls, you know, very good-looking girls, jolly-happy girls, and he wanted them to have a good time, and he's a good time. He was a nice fellow, that Mr. Hearst. And 'cause he was lots of money, and we fussed around him, you know.

So he wanted to go camping up the Slocan Valley with the girls. So we went up with the girls with tents, and the pony boys with the horses, you know. Went up the trail, and they took me along to go on the ice and they wanted to stay out that night.

Well, anyway, we went with the horses up there and to the last timber. And we saw a bear, way up on the slide. We showed him to the girls, and time went on. We went up there and made camp and made a huge fire, you know, and had dinner.

And it got clouded over and it was quite dark and it looked like a big storm coming on. So we sing a song there, and it was soon time to go to bed. As soon as it gets dark you go to bed, those things in the summer it's ten and after.

So, I was standing there by the fires, and the girls disappeared and then finally Mr. Hearst disappeared, and I stood there with the fire, smoking a little bit, you know, nice and quiet… figuring out the next day to go up onto the ice, and so here comes Mr. Hearst, running back.

He says, "Ed!"

"Yes, Mr. Hearst. What's wrong?"

"I tell you, the girls are all scared. They don't like to—they're scared in the tent of that bear they saw. They think the bear will come around. Would you mind sleeping with the girls, there?"

I says to Mr. Hearst, "A great pleasure, Mr. Hearst, in the mountains, to sleep with the girls!"

So I went in there, and it was a nice peaceful night, you know. There wasn't a thing around. There were six girls, yes, yes.

Oh, Just Some Place To Go

IVOR GUEST

*and the Journey from
Vancouver to South Fort George*

(RECORDED JULY 16, 1964)

IVOR GUEST (b. 1886) was born in Yarmouth, Nova Scotia, and went west to Edmonton in 1908 before coming to Vancouver prior to the winter of 1910. Like Arthur Shelford, he came West during trying economic times, with no wife or family, to find a lifestyle that suited him more than the one he was living on the East Coast. Guest tells the story about his trip from Vancouver with his two brothers up to Fort George.

Fort George was established in 1807 by Simon Fraser and served as a fur-trading post for the North West Company. The fort was established in the heart of Lheidli T'enneh First Nation land, and the relationship between Natives and newcomers is a central feature of Guest's anecdote. Guest remarks that it was in Fort George that he had his first-ever dealings with "Indians." Yet, the Native people of this area would have been dealing with newcomers for over 100 years by this time.

The post remained isolated during the Cariboo gold rush until 1906, when the Grand Trunk Pacific Railroad was established nearby. In 1909, development of the town began to pick up as two main townsites developed: South Fort George, which is on the Fraser River, and Central Fort George, which is nearly three kilometres away on the Nechako River. By 1913, each municipality had a population of around fifteen hundred people, as railway workers made the area a commercial hub. In 1915, four communities merged to form the city of Prince George, which is now the largest city in northern British Columbia.

FACING: *A Native woman with a dugout canoe,
near Fort George.* Photo: HP022168

Guest describes the road from Vancouver to South Fort George in 1911 as bustling with activity. Freight was transported all over the country, often using jerklines, teams of up to fourteen horses or mules tied in a line to pull three or four wagons. Stopping houses established along the freight roads drew teamsters (the people who drove the wagon trains) and travellers and were often filled with great storytellers and interesting characters.

Guest staked his land in 1912 near Fort George while working for the B.C. Forestry. After serving in the First World War, he received a Crown Grant for his land at Fort McLeod (now McLeod Lake), where he lived the rest of his life. He worked in the area, serving as a game warden as well as farming and working with furs, and was reputed to always be up for an adventure.

. . .

CD1, TRACK 8

ORCHARD: What did you come to Vancouver for? What did you—what was out there?

GUEST: Oh, just some place to go, and I worked there that winter [for the Eastman Kodak Company on Granville Street] and I saw posters of Fort George—how they could grow wheat and oranges, or not oranges, but peaches and apples, and so on.

So I thought, boy, that's a wonderful valley. I'll go up there. And I wrote to my brother in New York and told him where I was going, and he got kind of enthusiastic over this trip and he came out. And our younger brother was in the Bank of Montreal. He got a month's vacation and he came out.

We went to Ashcroft, bought a team of horses. That was May 1911. And we got a team of horses and a wagon, put our belongings in it and started for South Fort George, or Fort George. And we done—the team looked all right and the wagon, far as we knew. We weren't horsemen, I wasn't. And we got along about ten, twelve miles [nineteen kilometres] from town. One horse begin to make a funny noise. So I didn't know what it was, and we gave him a drink of water and the further we went, the more noise he made.

A jerkline team on the Cariboo Road near Ashcroft, 1909. Photo: HP010587

So a fella came along, McMullin, with a jerkline outfit. They had all the, the teamsters then had, they called jerklines—three teams and a leader. So he came along and I said, "Look, what's the matter with this horse?" I knew he'd know. So he stopped and he looked.

"Oh," he said, "that's so-and-so horse," (he named him). He said, "He's got the heaves."

"Well," I said, "what do you do for that?"

"Well," he said, "you can't do anything for it. Just take it easy and he'll do all right."

So we went along with the heave-y horse all the way through to Fort George, but all along the way there were many of these jerkline outfits. All the freight went in with horses then. There wasn't a car. We didn't see a car, of course, no trucks, all the time we were on the way. And we went all along through and stopped at these roadhouses. And they, well, we usually took a tent and tented out but we did stop a time or two, and the teamsters would come in and there'd be a bunch of men there and there'd be a great big poker game going on, right away. And, of course, a certain amount of liquor, but nobody got drunk.

But they had some wonderful big roadhouses: The Hundred Mile and Ninety-Five and Hundred and Fifty, and so on. And they all stopped at these roadhouses. The men would stop and they'd sleep and eat there and the horses were put up and fed.

Well, that went on until we got to Quesnel, and at Quesnel they had a ferry, and a fellow was running the ferry across the river; he took us over. And we started for, that was the last leg of—to Fort George. And the road, it was a very, very poor road. And after we crossed the Blackwater River [West Road River], the road was just slashed out through the timber. No road at all. And it was pretty hard going and no feed, of course, and no place to buy any.

So we, it was in around the first of May, it was a nice spring, nice weather, and there was a little grass but we'd have to take the horses way down someplace where we could find grass. And we finally got into South Fort George; the first day of May 1911.

Well, there was, what, two, I think there're two white women there then. Mrs. John McInnis was there, and John [who ran for office in Fort George in 1916]; Mrs. McLaughlin and another lady there. And, of course, on the hill they had some other women at different times but that's all there was in South at that time.

Well, we had quite a time to feed the horses. I went to get oats, and oats was twelve cents a pound, and I got fifty cents worth in a little sack and gave each of the horses a feed, all there was in that. And, of course, I made up my mind right then, we had to get rid of these horses.

Well, we looked for feed, and the Indians told us there was some grass down here where Prince George is today, down on George Street. So we took the horses down there and put them on the grass. And the next day a man came over and he said, "I'd like to buy one of the horses." So I says, "I want to sell the team."

"No," he says, "I just want one." So I said, "Alright, I'll sell you one."

So he paid me enough for the one horse that we paid for the both of them, so I didn't make any loss. So he bought the horses—$225 for this old horse I had.

And an Indian came along and he said, "I'd like to trade a canoe for this horse." Well, I didn't want the horse. They were a nuisance. You had to keep watching them. I said, "Sure!"

So he brought over a canoe. We were camped on the Fraser, and they were just above us in the Indian village and he came down with the canoe and said, "Look, nice new canoe."

Well, it looked good to me. And he put the canoe up on the beach and a couple of paddles and two traps he said, "I throw in." Well, that's fine. So I said, "The horse, you know where he is." So he got the horse.

I went uptown and met a fella, Livingstone, Ernie Livingstone. He was from back in Yarmouth, Nova Scotia. And I told him how I traded the horse.

He said, "You traded for canoe?"

I said, "Yes."

He said, "That canoe, I know, is no good." He said, "Who traded?" He says, "Paulette." Or I told him, "Paulette."

"Oh," he says, "I know it's no good."

"Oh," I said, "looks good. Brand new and nice shape, everything."

So we went down and looked. He looked at it, and the first thing he said, "I *knew* it was no good."

"Well," I said, "what's wrong with it?"

"Well," he said, "see that split in the bow and the split in the stern?" He said, "It's gonna have two halves, that'll just break right in two."

"Well," I said, "by golly! I'll fix that up. I'll put tin on it."

He said, "You can't put enough tin on there to hold it. It's gonna split."

And sure enough, the thing, in the water and out the water. I tried to keep it wet, and it come out and it just broke in two. So that was about a week after I traded, it broke right in two, two pieces.

So the Indian came back. He said, "Ooh," he said, "that no good." He said, "Horse die."

"Well," I said, "you can have the canoe back."

He said—and he laughed. He said, "Both stung!"

So that was my first dealings with the Indians.

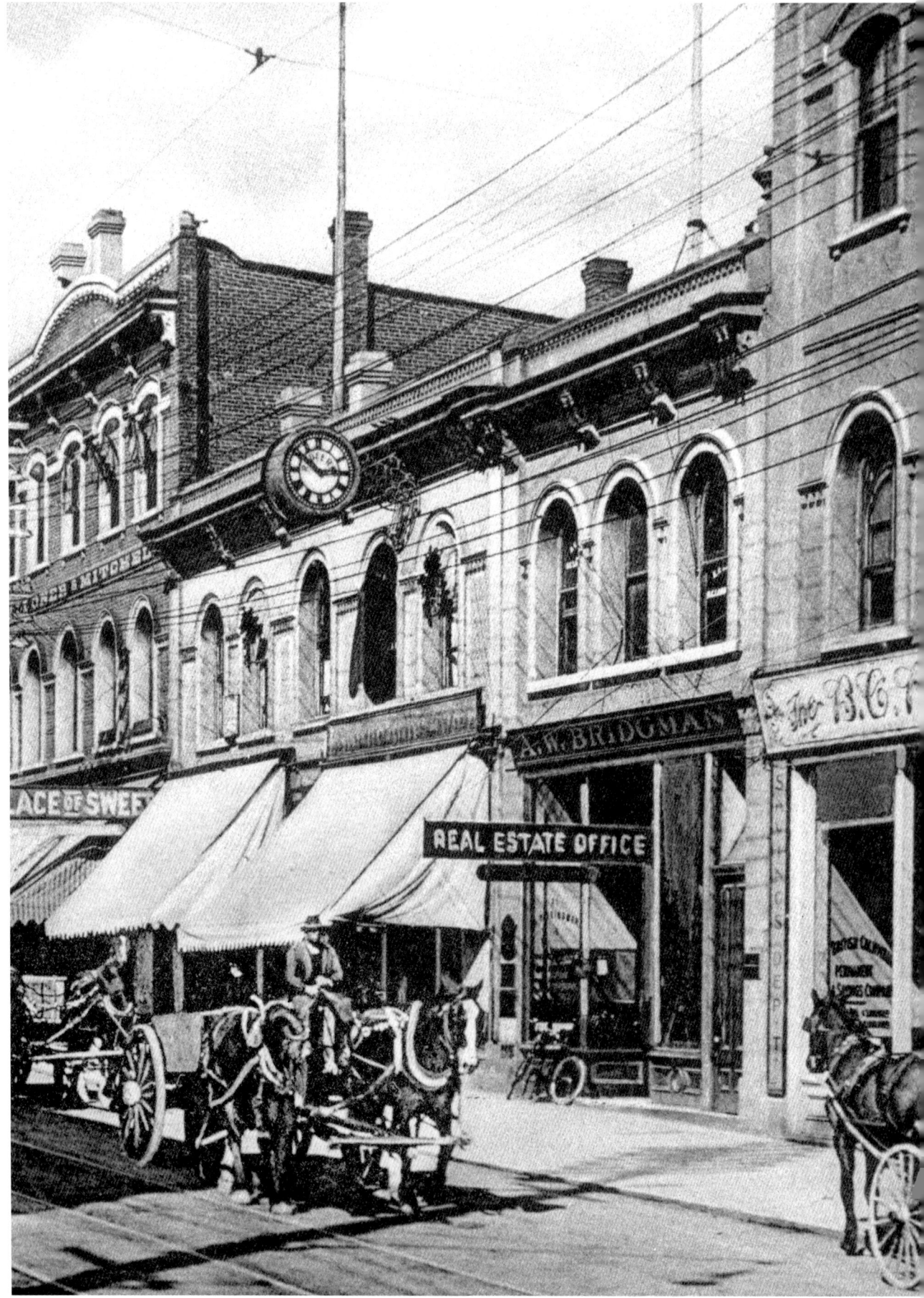

(3)

The Growth of New Cities

In 1911, only four cities in British Columbia had populations over four thousand: Nanaimo (8,306), New Westminster (13,199), Victoria (31,660) and Vancouver (100,401). This chapter features two stories about what life was like in the 1890s in two of British Columbia's fast-growing cities: Victoria and Vancouver. These stories offer a window into life in these locales during their infancy, well before they grew into the cities they are today.

In 1841, James Douglas chose the area where Victoria is now as the ideal location to set up a Hudson's Bay trading post. The Coast Salish people had been living in the area for thousands of years and had cleared large plots of land to grow camas flowers, a staple food and source of starch. Upon viewing these fields, experiencing the mild climate and sailing into the calm harbour, Douglas declared the location "a perfect Eden."

FACING: *Government Street, Victoria, 1908.*
Photo: *HP002195*

In the early days of the gold rush, Douglas passed a law that all immigrants had to pass through Victoria to get a licence before venturing out to the goldfields. Thus, Victoria became a commercial hub literally overnight as the population jumped from five hundred people to more than five thousand, thereby becoming western Canada's oldest city. Then, when British Columbia joined Confederation in 1871, Victoria became the capital of the new province.

One of the terms of Confederation was that the transcontinental railway should end in Victoria. Millions of dollars were spent trying to figure out how to get the rail line to Victoria, but in the end the idea was deemed unrealistic. As an alternative, it was decided that the terminus would be in Burrard Inlet on the mainland, and as a result, Vancouver grew rapidly from a small logging-and-lumber-mill settlement to the largest city in western Canada in 1887. That year, when the railway arrived in Vancouver, Victoria lost its place as the commercial hub of the province.

Horse and Buggy Days

ROGER MONTEITH

and Victoria in the 1890s

(RECORDED MARCH, 1962)

A VETERAN of the First World War, Major Roger Monteith (1885–1966) was born and raised, and lived his whole life in Victoria. His father was an administrator in the city and had a family consisting of four sons and two daughters. The major himself owned and operated a tackle shop on Fort Street. His intimate familiarity with the city is clearly demonstrated by the detailed and nuanced recollections he shares in the following anecdote.

The Victoria depicted by Monteith is that of the 1890s: a community-based area with a strong Native and Chinese presence, where life moved at a slow pace and drinking was a central aspect of social life. He also recalls The Birdcages, the first government buildings from 1859 that were replaced in the 1890s by the current provincial Parliament Buildings. All of the street names and one bar that Monteith mentions still exist to this day.

. . .

MONTEITH: I was born here on January 4th, 1885. I can visualize Victoria back, far as 1890. It seemed to me that the city, in those days, all centred on Government Street. That was the only business street in town in those days, that is, the retail section. I will say that there was a certain amount of the smaller stores on Yates Street and Fort Street, up as far as Douglas, but there it ended.

CD2, TRACK 1

ABOVE: *The Garrick's Head Saloon, with owner Thomas J. Burnes, ca. 1889. Photo: HP090236/Clyde Banfield Collection*

Douglas Street didn't amount to anything. In those days, with the exception of a few old hotels. Of course, you've got to remember that the traffic from Esquimalt came in over Point Ellice Bridge, and then via the old Rock Bay Bridge, along Store Street and up Johnson. That created a certain amount of retail business on lower Johnson: clothiers, the old Saunders Grocery, Shotbolt's Drug Store. They were all familiar old places in those days.

But as far as the actual business of the town concerned, it was all centred on Government Street. Of course, I'm talking of the days long before we ever thought of chain stores, *marketeeriers* [sic] or anything of that sort. It was all horse-and-buggy days. There were no motor cars. There were no street cars then. Everything was by horse-drawn vehicle.

Government Street extended, then, straight through, southwards, as far as the Johnson Street Bridge, long before the causeway. From the far side of the bridge, it extended on out into Beacon Hill Park but was then known as Birdcage Walk, the name being taken from the then government buildings. They were known as The Birdcages.

I remember The Birdcages well. They looked like a collection of Chinese pagodas.

ORCHARD: Why did they make them that shape, I wonder?

MONTEITH: I can't tell you. The last one only burnt down a few years ago. They had it as a historical relic back of the Parliament Buildings but, unfortunately, just a few years ago, the thing burned down.

There was a group of them there, on the side of the present Parliament Buildings. Now then, as I've said, those were the horse-and-buggy days. It is very interesting to see the hack stands [taxi stands] and the express-cart stands along Government Street in that block between Yates Street and Government, you'd see the hacks drawn up.

It was very seldom a cabby in sight there. You had to go into the nearest pub to retrieve him. They put in hours of waiting for fares and they killed time by going into the nearest pub, of which there were many. And very often you'd have to go in and call for your cabby, but if you had some particular cabby that you wanted to engage and he didn't happen to be the first in line, say the second or third or fourth, you got an earful from the other cabby who, ahead of him there. And the same way with the drays, as we called them, horse-drawn vehicles for freighting, on Yates Street and on Wharf Street. They just waited by the hour there, for fares, and you had to retrieve them from the pubs.

Talking of pubs, in those days, why, it seemed to me there was a bar on every corner. Very often, one between whiles. Of course, those were totally different days we lived in. I mean, they were days of easy going, you might say. People took their time. We had more time to stop and talk to your friends. You'd meet somebody on the street that you knew, you'd stop and have a few words with them instead of just nodding and going by.

Well, that very, very often led to a suggestion from one or the other, well, let's go and have a drink. And there was nearly always a bar at your elbow, whether it was the Brown Jug, The Grotto, the Garrick's Head, and you'd go in and have a drink.

Drinks in those days were two for a quarter, I might say. Any drink you wanted, outside of, well, I mean something like champagne or some expensive thing, but any drink you wanted and there was no such thing as a jigger on the bottles to measure your drink. You'd call for your brand of Scotch or rye, whatever you wanted. The bottle was placed on the bar in front of you. You poured out what you'd want: one finger, two fingers, half a glassful. And as I say, they ran two for a quarter, so your drinks didn't amount to very much.

Another custom was, if two or three of you went in for a drink there, well, you nearly all bought a drink each, and it is a usual thing to ask the bartender to have one with you. Well, he'd had quite a few, he'd explain, but he'd have a little drop of his own. He'd have a bottle of cold tea there, or else he'd take a cigar. Then when you got through, a decent barkeeper would always reciprocate: "Well, now have one on me, boys!"

I can remember that, one occasion, we got a rather snooty bartender who didn't reciprocate. The bottle's on the bar. We waited and waited and waited, and he didn't suggest we have a drink on the house. The man on the end of the bar took a bottle off the bar, held it down below the level of the bar, filled his glass up and then passed it on, still below the level of the bar to the next man. So we all got our free drink that way!

Inside the Sunnyside Cash Grocery Store, 106 Fort Street, ca. 1890s. Photo: HP053524

I don't want you to think that we spent our lives in bars, but that was a great part of the life in those days, the bars!

The stores, I can remember well. Totally different to what you have today. There were no glass cases in those days, showcases. There was nothing in the way of refrigeration. Everything was put out openly. There'd be hams and bacon and generally barrels of English biscuits mixed, currants, raisins, huge cheeses and a variety of other things—including, as a rule, a coffee grinder, where they ground your coffee as you wanted it. The consequence was those places had a most enticing odour to them of all these different provisions there. You were entitled to sample any of them—the biscuits or the raisins and that sort of thing.

Then the butcher shops, the same way. They had no refrigeration. All the meats were hung out in the open. There was no refrigeration, and you'd see entire carcasses of beef and hogs, lamb and sheep there. And you'd go in there and order the particular joint you want off the particular carcass.

I might say that beef in those days, to the best of my recollection, was about eight cents a pound, and you got really well-aged beef, not like today when it's under refrigeration.

Christmas time, those places were a great sight. They'd have, on show outside, an entire carcass, a huge great bullock there—I couldn't say what he weighed—and the other pillar opposite the doorway there'd be an equally huge pig—probably weighed about half a ton. And there were turkeys and various other things. It made quite a show!

Christmas time came—your grocer and your butcher generally gave the big families a turkey or a sucking [sic] pig or a goose or something of that nature. You never had to buy your Christmas turkey. I don't know how the butchers and the grocers financed in those days, but it was common practice for the big family to pay their bill, maybe half yearly, or maybe quarterly. You'd get a bill for, maybe, three hundred to four hundred dollars, but that was commonly done. How they financed, I don't know, because you had no finance companies of any sort in those days. I presume that the banks looked after them, but no questions asked and no interest was charged. No, no, we never thought of interest. That was clean out.

The streets in those days were always quite a problem. In winter, of course, there was no paving in those days, never thought of, and the sidewalks, even on Government Street were boards, laid crossways. I've seen grass growing through them on Government Street, and the horses nibbling away at this grass growing. The consequence was that during the winter months, in the rain, they were a sea of mud. There was always a small crew of city workmen scraping this mud into little mounds, and you had to be very careful, before they were carted away, that you didn't wade through these about up to your knees.

Then, come summer, there was then just a sea of dust. The watering carts used to go around, water them up and down the main streets, maybe twice a day. And—but that didn't always alleviate the dust, because in about half an hour it was all dried up again. There were horses everywhere. You'd see horses tied up to hitching posts, or else with these weights they used on the end of a halter, and the horse would nibble 'round and you'd see the grass actually growing up there.

Now the banks on the corner where the Bank of Commerce is now, that was originally the Bank of British Columbia, and incidentally that's where I entered business life. I joined the Bank of British Columbia in October 1899, and I'm one of the only two surviving members of that date.

There were a lot of banks in those days here that have gradually been absorbed, that don't exist. There was Molson's Bank, the Merchants Bank of Halifax, there was a Northern Bank, afterwards the Northern Crown. There was a Bank of BNA, and there were several others I just cannot recollect now, but they were gradually all absorbed.

While I'm talking of banks, I might mention that the Bank of Commerce took over the Bank of British Columbia on January 1st, 1900. I continued on, of course, with the Bank of British Columbia. Incidentally, I might say that I started in, my salary was the large sum of $14.86 a month.

The days I've been describing Government Street and Johnson Street, there were many Indians here then. The reserve, the main reserve of the Songhees, was on the other side of Johnson Street Bridge, what is now known as the industrial reserve, with the Sidney Roofing Paper Company on it. That was all Indian reserve then. And you'd see the Indians coming in every day, nearly always in bare feet, sometimes with a bag of clams, other times with a sack with a couple of salmon in it.

Another thing, in those days, that was a very familiar sight were the Chinese peddlers. They went in for peddling fish and vegetables and then collecting old bottles and then chickens they would buy from us. They'd wander miles afield. They'd have a bamboo pole with a basket on each end, and they're always careful to balance up the weight on both ends. And as they jog-trotted along, the poles would bend, up and down like this, and they'd set their pace to the jogging of this pole and they could go for miles, hours, at a jog-trot, with a big weight in them. I've lifted some of them to feel the weight of them, but it's that peculiar gait they used that eased the weight on their shoulders.

They would call on the various houses, with vegetables, and then there'd be a fish man with, maybe, halibut or salmon or something, and a big board and a big knife. He'd call at the house and would cut you off whatever you wanted. It was very cheap, and it was the only way you got it in those days because there were no regular callers of vegetables, no proper vegetable shops. There were fish shops, I will say.

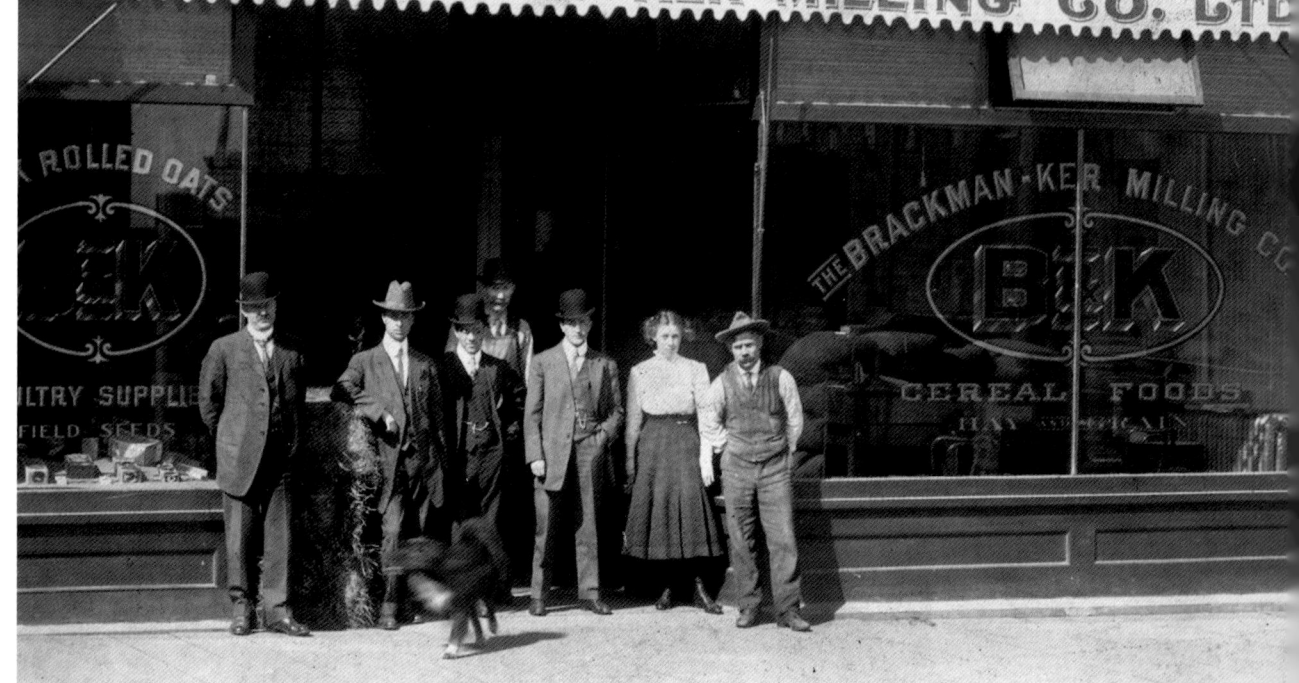

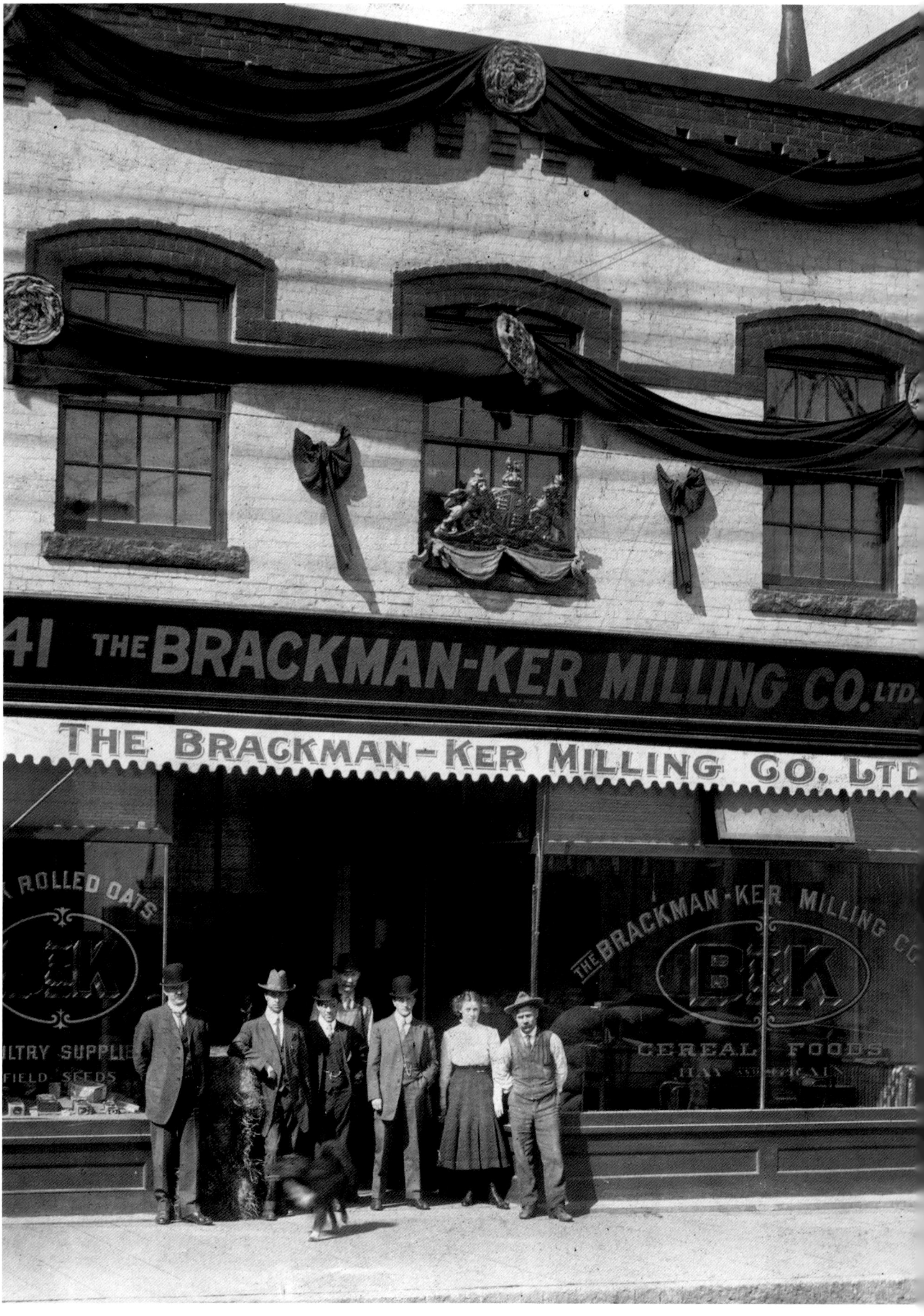

41 THE BRACKMAN-KER MILLING CO. LTD.
THE BRACKMAN-KER MILLING CO. LTD
ROLLED OATS
THE BRACKMAN-KER MILLING
B&K
CEREAL FOODS

The Town Was Changing So Fast

ISABEL SWEENY

on Early Days in Vancouver

(RECORDED SEPTEMBER 1967)

THE CHARMING Isabel Sweeny (1889–1974) discusses how her father worked for the Canadian Pacific Railway (CPR) before settling in Vancouver in 1885. In the process she gives wonderful details of what life was like in the city of Vancouver in its first few years, as it began to grow into the largest city in British Columbia.

Sweeny's father, Henry Ogle Bell-Irving (1856–1931), a Scot who was trained as an engineer in Germany, came to British Columbia in 1882 to survey the Rocky Mountains for the CPR. He arrived at the Burrard Inlet lumber village of Granville in October 1885, five months before it was renamed Vancouver—after Captain George Vancouver—and just the second European to enter Burrard Inlet. In 1890, Bell-Irving founded the Anglo–British Columbia Packing Company, which made him a very wealthy man, as it became the largest salmon exporter on the west coast. In fact, by April 1891, the company had bought nine other canneries on the Fraser and Skeena rivers and produced over one-quarter of British Columbia's salmon pack. At the time of his death in 1931, he was ranked the sixteenth-wealthiest man in Vancouver: his estate had a net worth of $399,000.

The city of Vancouver developed quickly from a small lumber town to a fast-growing city: from a population of 1,000 in 1881, to 20,000 by 1900, and 100,000 by 1911. Sweeny mentions The Great Vancouver Fire of 1886, which killed dozens of people, caused 1.3 million dollars

FACING: *Brackman-Ker Milling Co., Vancouver, 1898.*
Photo: *I-68536*

of damage and destroyed most of the city. On June 13 of that year, city workers set a fire to clear land between Main and Cambie streets; however, a strong gale caused the blaze to burn out of control. Within days, though, houses were being raised and the city was being rebuilt with infrastructure for streetcars, electricity and clean water. As well, she recalls when the village of Sun'ahk, a Native village established in 1839, was displaced to Squamish from Vancouver in 1901. A 372-square-metre longhouse sat under what is now the Burrard Street Bridge and was surrounded by houses, a cemetery and several orchards.

In this story, Sweeny offers insight into life in the city when it was still a sparsely populated settlement around the turn of the twentieth century.

. . .

CD2, TRACK 2

ORCHARD: What was your father's name?

SWEENY: Henry Ogle Bell-Irving. And he was an engineer and he came with the building of the CPR, taking it on at Winnipeg and he was with them until the Great Divide.

ORCHARD: What was your father planning to do in coming out here?

SWEENY: He was with the advance party—the advance survey party coming through, finding the way through. Actually, he never was pleased at the positioning of the first way through because, you know, they had to hurry up over some contract they had, a mail contract. And they were working for time and eventually when they put in the Rogers Pass and different things, they made the grade better. You see, it was terribly steep at that time.

I remember, as young children, going over the mountains and we had one going up where the Rogers Pass tunnel goes now. We had one engine in the front, two in the middle and one at the back, and these great big wood-burners with wide open mouths.

But he fell in love with this part [Vancouver] and decided this was where he wanted to live. And he made his way back to England and brought my—married my mother, and they came out by ship to the southern states and across the southern states to California, from there, up to Victoria, and from Victoria over to New Westminster by the old paddlewheel steamer, *Yosemite*.

They were here during the fire and, now since you think of that, I remember Mother telling me that they watched the fire, eventually they were out in a little boat out in the harbour watching. Of course, they'd done everything they could, and all the lumber for the new home and all Daddy's engineering tools and everything of that sort, all his instruments were burnt. Everything was burnt. And, as you know, there was quite a loss of life in that fire.

I was born in '89. I can remember those first years. I have a very vivid memory of some of the things that happened those first years. The town was changing so very, very, very fast, and railway tracks and shunting areas and all the rest of the excitement down there, it was no longer a nice place to be.

I remember Granville Street. I remember when the big hotel was built and I can remember leaning out of our nursery window on Seton Street, listening to the frogs—terrific amount of frogs at nighttime, and that's where the courthouse now is. That was a swamp. I do remember that.

ORCHARD: Now they've got a fountain there.

SWEENY: Now they've got a fountain instead of frogs, yes, yes.

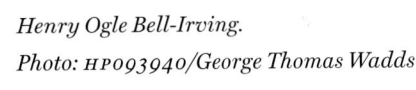

Henry Ogle Bell-Irving.
Photo: HP093940/George Thomas Wadds

I do remember riding, with my father, out over South Granville. We had to cross, there was one bridge across, and we—riding out over the hill, about by 16th. A bear and her cub crossed the road, and my pony went into the ditch on one side and Father's into the ditch on the other, and that was just a little thin forest road.

The West End, I can remember—I'll make you laugh—some of my brothers wanted to go camping. And they said firmly they didn't want to camp anywhere near, they wanted to go to somewhere that was really

*The Kitsilano First Nation in a scow being relocated to Squamish Reserve, 1901.
Photo: PN08924*

decently wild. So they went, and a couple of days afterwards my dad and I went to see if they were still alive and we crossed over the West End, the main part where all the apartment houses are now, over a little tiny bit of a trail, jumping over logs and whatnot, and we came out to where we found their camp. And it was at English Bay. And that's absolutely true. And they were nearly dead with sunburn, I remember.

You could take a boat from there and go out to a place, which we afterwards knew as Jericho Beach. And my father and uncle used to go out there to play golf, and there was no dyke then at all. It was tidal.

And we children were taken along. Some of us were taken along. For a day's trip it felt like going to California for the distance. We were the ball finders because they just played among the logs in the sand. And then, you see, later on, they dyked it all and then they made the beautiful country club we had there later on.

Oh, and that brings me to a story which I think is really rather nice. Later on, when we were living high up on the top of north Lonsdale, a Mrs. Jim Abbott, who had been an Alexander in the days when we lived on Alexander Street, came up to visit me up there. And we were telling old tales, and I thought I had an awfully good one to tell her about our going out with Daddy to find the balls out among the logs at Jericho.

And she said, "I can do better than that." She said, "I can remember going out to Jericho from Alexander Street with my father, via the narrows and in an Indian canoe, paddled by Indians."

Now that really is an unusual one, isn't it?

I can also remember the Indians that used to come to us from the Moodyville Village, the village now in North Vancouver village, in canoes, and they'd bring us blackberries.

I can remember watching and being aware that I was watching history. I was pretty young. I suppose I was about 18.

There was an Indian village on the—where there is now a marina on the—where there used to be air force buildings, and now there's a marina underneath, on the west side of the bridge, of the Burrard Bridge. That was the last Indian village that was, they moved the Indians and I hope that they paid them well and everything was happy. This I don't know.

But they felt that it was not right for them to be living so completely in the middle of the town as they were. They were practically under the Burrard Bridge on that little area beside Kitsilano Park, which was afterwards given to the city.

I remember very well, the day, early in the morning, two tugs came in at very high tide and pushed the tugs, the scows high up the beaches as far as possible. And all day long, the Indians in that little community were going to and fro. From where I was, you could only see them like little figures moving to and fro, taking all their belongings onto the scows.

The evening came and the sun set, and the tugs came in again, and I can remember feeling, that is something, real history happening in my day. The last of the Indians living in our neighbourhood are moving, and they went up to Squamish. They were taken up. Mind you, their land, their area, their chieftain will tell you that their area went up as far as Squamish anyway, that was part of their land anyway. And I think, I hope, that it was properly done, you know, that they were properly paid for it. But it was a matter of—the Indians set fire to the cottages before they left. And this I remember very, very well.

(4)

Working Out West

Mining, ranching, prospecting, canning, mountaineering, packing and many other jobs helped to keep British Columbia's economy moving and growing in the years before the First World War. Many of these resources were located in remote places, which meant that people had to immerse themselves in new and unfamiliar lifestyles. They often had to build their own communities and survive in harsh conditions, just to earn a living.

Gold miners were the first non-Native workers to establish a strong presence in B.C.; however, gold mining was just the first of the many rugged vocations people had to endure out West. In addition to a couple of gold-mining tales, this chapter also contains two detailed stories

FACING: *The Canadian Pacific Railway in Rogers Pass, ca. 1897. Photo: CP-0004* about life building the railroads and working in the sealing industry. All of these jobs involved dangerous conditions, often backbreaking and uncomfortable work, and long unpredictable hours, but many British Columbians still made these jobs into lifelong careers. They relished the uncertainty and the adventure that came from working in British Columbia's unpredictable land and seascapes.

Gold Was Lying on Top of the Ground

ARTIE PHAIR

and the Lillooet Gold Rush

(RECORDED JULY 26, 1964)

THE FRASER Canyon gold rush is significant in the history of this province not only because of the population boom it created but also because it led to the declaration of the Colony of British Columbia. With so many new people in what was formally known as the fur-trading district of New Caledonia, the British felt they needed to assert authority in the region, especially since the Oregon Treaty of 1846 between Britain and the U.S. had left the area unincorporated. The district was converted to a Crown colony called British Columbia, and the then Governor of Vancouver Island, James Douglas, was also made governor of the Colony of British Columbia in 1858.

When the first rumours of gold surfaced, Douglas had the foresight to restrict immigration to the new British colony by requiring that anyone wanting to search for gold or work in the goldfields on the mainland first obtain a licence in Victoria. As a result, thousands of people from a variety of ethnicities, languages and cultures passed through the city as they scrambled to get to the goldfields to fulfill their dreams of unlimited wealth. Although many of the miners were unsuccessful, in their rush most had no care for the environment, the indigenous people or even for anyone aside from their immediate partners. Despite the licences, Douglas had little means to set up infrastructure or enforce laws quickly from all the way over in Victoria. In fact, in 1858, the gold rush city of Yale was known as hub of depravity, violence and lawlessness.

ABOVE: *The Golden Cache Mine of Lillooet was built on the face of a cliff, 1897.* Photo: HP009656

Arthur "Artie" William A. Phair (1880–1967) was the first non-Native person born in Lillooet, and with the exception of a few years as a teenager while he attended school in Victoria, he lived his entire life there. The Phair family had settled in the area in 1862, and they hunted, fished and raised sheep for years while spending a lot of time working with various Aboriginal people. Phair ran the family store and served as coroner, archivist and local photographer; he was the foremost expert on the gold rushes in the area, as his father, Caspar Phair (d. 1933) was Lillooet's first gold commissioner.

. . .

PHAIR: There were really no whites here [in Lillooet] until the gold rush of 1858. Well, then the Indians, they were living just as they had lived for twenty thousand years, they claim. They could never adjust themselves really, to the white man's way of living.

The earlier history was this: that in about 1856, gold was found around Yale but they didn't think much of it. The first people that came up the Fraser River, they didn't think much of it or they could make ten, twenty dollars a day but that wasn't very much in those days. And they kept up the canyon until they got to Lytton. And that's where the first fellows made a big mistake.

Instead of coming up the Fraser River, they went up the Thompson River and they landed way out in Alberta. So they condemned the country and said not much.

But in 1858, the news had got out to California. Before that, there were no white people in here at all. It was all Indians and the Hudson's Bay [Company], but they weren't very strong here because it wasn't very good fur country. They owned the—around Stuart Lake, up in the Cariboo. That was their headquarters, you see.

ORCHARD: That was the Hudson Bay?

PHAIR: The Hudson Bay. They really owned the whole country but they didn't think much of this country, you see. And when they heard of this gold here, Governor Douglas was in charge of the country, and he really tried to keep it quiet because he knew that the minute Californians found out there was gold here, they did, they came up here. Some people say there were sixty thousand people came in here. I know there was anywhere from thirty to forty, fifty thousand.

Then Governor Douglas, in 1858, when he heard they were coming up, and he gave Otis Parsons [a noted miner in the Cariboo region] a contract to build a road from Harrison Lake up to Lillooet. So they could get up the Fraser River. You couldn't get up the canyon above Lytton, you remember.

Anyway, Governor Douglas gave Otis Parsons a contract, and I think Otis Parsons had five hundred men. I had Otis Parsons' diary and I copied it all but I think I lost it in the fire. But anyway, it's in the archives now. Luckily I sent it there and they've got—you can get copies of it then.

Anyway, this trail was built and then, of course, all the miners came up to Lillooet. They mined out Yale in about a year, they took all the gold out there. Then they came up to Lillooet and when they struck Lillooet here, some of them made from a hundred dollars to five hundred dollars a day, just panning around the river here. The gold was lying on top of the ground really.

They had as many as four thousand rockers, I believe, because all these bars had gold laying on top of them really. And I think at one time there was about four thousand people working here, and they were all making $50, maybe $100, up to $500.

Well, then they kept—they soon mined this up, maybe in two or three years. Well then, they kept moving up to Cariboo, you see. But Lillooet got to be a town of about seven thousand people here. At first, Lillooet was called Cayoosh. I don't know why. We don't know really what the Cayoosh means. And then when the whites came up here in '60, '59 and '60, they built quite a town here then.

As the miners went up the river, they found it richer and richer. And then they built this road from Lillooet to Cariboo. That's why the Mile 0 starts at Lillooet.

Well, by 1864, then, the people had built a road from Yale to Lytton, Spences Bridge, Ashcroft and joined our road to Clinton. Well, the effect of that was, it killed all the travel up this way through Harrison Lake and Lillooet Lake, and Lillooet became a ghost town. Everyone pulled out of here. And it was a ghost town until, for about twenty years. There was very little doing here, until in 1884, the Chinese, about three thousand Chinamen working on the CPR, you know, they were just about at the end of their contracts, see. Well, then those Chinamen, a lot of them started mining on the river. Well, they were satisfied with a dollar a day, along in there, a couple of dollars a day. And they came up to Lillooet here, six hundred of them, and instead of going up the river, they just thought they'd try Cayoosh Creek. About four miles from here, they found that there was a million dollars to every mile there for seven miles.

My father said there was at least seven million dollars taken out there in seven miles. And that was right up to the Golden Cache, but they never thought of looking up on the hill to see where it came from. And [Joe] Copeland just found it accidentally—didn't even know what gold was.

Captain Otis Parsons, one of the Cariboo's best-known miners. Photo: HP006780/Bradley and Rulofson

Well, then of course, the Chinamen, in two years, in two years they had the whole thing mined out and they moved out then. Well, then Lillooet became a ghost town again.

An ore train at the Bralorne Mine, 1937. Photo: HP059952

That was '84. Well, there was nothing happening then until, in '86, my father had a prospector out and he found gold opposite the Golden Cache but it wasn't very big. Very rich, but they didn't think much of it and they abandoned it. Well then, of course, the next boom was the Golden Cache and that, I think, started Lillooet.

In 1896, a half-breed called Copeland went up Cayoosh Creek here, and the Chinamen didn't know where all this gold came from, and Copeland happened to go up to the top of the mountain. He shot a goat, and the goat fell over a bluff there. And when Copeland looked at the bluff here, just a pile of rocks, he saw all this yellow stuff. He didn't know what it was and he brought down a specimen or two in his pocket and there was an engineer, a mining engineer, in camp having supper with them.

And the engineer looked at it and, "Oh," he said, "that's nothing. That's probably copper. It's just pretty." And he threw it away.

Well, Copeland's wife [Eliza] had been accustomed to panning on the river here. She knew what gold was, so she broke this rock up.

So she came to Copeland on the quiet and said, "Look here, Joe. That's gold!"

So the engineer knew it was gold. So then there was Copeland and this engineer who knew it was gold, and Copeland told his friends. He had another half-breed with him and a white man and a white man, you know they had two women too, two Indian women. Copeland had one, his wife.

So they watched this fellow. He said, "Boys, well, I'll—" he said, "Thanks very much for the meal. I think I'll go home now."

So they watched him going, and instead of going home, he started up the mountain. He was going to stake the claim, see. So, these two half-breeds, they got their guns and they went after this fellow. And they caught him just as he was going to start to stake this thing.

And they said, "You son-of-a-gun!" They probably used worse words than that. They said, "You get off this country or we'll shoot you right now, and we'll throw your body in the river here and there'll be no more of you!"

Well, of course, this engineer went home then, and the others, there was one white man with them, you see, with Copeland, and they couldn't read or write. So they made a proposition to this white man, Arthur Noel. (He got to be famous after a while in mining.)

They said, "Now, if you'll stake four claims there, two for Copeland, one for Larry Shell and one for yourself," he says, "We'll give you one of the claims."

So Arthur Noel went up and staked these claims for the boys. They brought some of their nuggets down, came down to town here, and there were two men in town here. Of course, Arthur Noel was a white man and he spoke to them. He kind of knew them, I think.

He said, "Look here!" he said, "They've got something there worthwhile."

It was Colonel MacKinnon of Vancouver and [Howard] DeBeck of [New] Westminster.

So Colonel MacKinnon said, "I'll tell you what I'll do, boys. I'll give you twenty-five thousand cash, right now, without even looking at it."

The boys took the twenty-five thousand dollars.

ORCHARD: The boys? That's the two half-breeds?

PHAIR: The half-breeds. The two half-breeds and Arthur Noel. So that was like a million dollars in those days.

Well, Larry Shell, he didn't go back to the claim but he took and put this six thousand dollars in his pocket and went down to Vancouver, and they found his body in the harbour the next day. Somebody had killed him, see, for his six thousand dollars. You know, in those days there were no banks or anything. He was just a kid, you know. And they fixed him.

Well, then Copeland and Arthur Noel... Arthur Noel became manager, and they ran some tunnels into this thing and here's where the crooked work starts.

So they formed a company, ten cents a share, a million shares I think it was. And the shares went up to three dollars a share. And they ran tunnels into this mountain and when they got in about a hundred feet [thirty metres], there was no more gold. You know, it had played out. It often does that in mining.

So after they knew it was no good, they sent out reports, had the mining engineer report that this mountain was gold. And the shares went up to three dollars a share. You know, they're doing it today, the same thing. So it was one of the greatest booms; it started Lillooet. There were probably a thousand miners in here, came in from all over the country. And that was the first time Lillooet really started to be a town.

These stocks were sold all over the country, in London even. But an old man came out from London here and he looked at it, and they fooled him and told him it was a mountain of gold and he believed it, you know. It was one of the darnedest swindles in the country, you know.

ORCHARD: What was the name of the mine?

PHAIR: They called it the Golden Cache. Well then, of course, everything was staked for twenty and thirty miles around it. There were thousands of claims staked. They staked all these mountains around here and if you went—now, my friend had a claim up here, he had it bought for ten thousand dollars. And my father had a claim next door and they offered him eight thousand dollars.

"No," he says. "I want ten thousand for it because Copeland gave it to me. He got something out of it."

Oh, they just went crazy. And then when they—just the opposite then—when they found there was nothing there, just everything dropped. But it led to the finding—see then people, these prospectors went away up Bridge River, and it led to them finding the Bralorne Mine.

You've heard of Bralorne, of course, haven't you? That's one of the biggest gold mines in the country, you see. That's been running for fifty or sixty years. I suppose they've taken out, oh probably a hundred million dollars or more. I remember the time Bralorne took out four million a year. The find was made in 1896 and it didn't boom until about 1898, and in a couple of years, by about 1899, the country was, they'd found out and everybody pulled out of the country.

And, of course, it led to the finding of the Bralorne, and from then on Lillooet got to be a little town, you know. It improved slowly until— and the next boom, of course, was the building of the PG [Prince George] railway. Because, of course, before we had a railway in here you couldn't do anything with these mines. But when the railway came in, of course, and then, well, things gradually improved, you know.

I'll Sell It To You Cheap

GUS MILLIKEN

and the Hills Bar Claim

(RECORDED MARCH 13, 1963)

THE FRASER Canyon gold rush brought the first intense wave of non-Native immigration to the region around 1858. Just nine years prior, in 1849, tens of thousands of people, American and others, had flocked to California for that area's rush and were based in San Francisco awaiting word of the next gold boom. When news got out that gold had been found in British Columbia, around where the Thompson and Fraser rivers meet, miners raced to Yale and Lytton and began to pan the banks of the rivers between and around these two locales. In the seventy-six kilometres between these two towns were many thriving Aboriginal communities, whose lifestyles were greatly interrupted and adversely affected by the impact of the gold rush.

August "Gus" Milliken was a prominent historian and photographer from Yale, which is located on the banks of the Fraser River, right above where the water in the canyon starts to churn and currents pick up as the river begins its rush to the Pacific Ocean. Sternwheelers heading inland up the Fraser River were forced to stop at Yale, and eventually the wagon road to the Cariboo goldfields began there. In 1858, the population had swelled to over thirty thousand, many of whom staked claims at Hills Bar. Situated just outside Yale, this bar was the first in the area to be mined, and it was also the richest.

Milliken uncovered artifacts that proved that First Nations had inhabited the area up to nine thousand years ago, and Milliken Site, an

FACING: *Fort Yale became a significant gold mining town after the discovery at Hills Bar.*
Photo: HP094525/Frederick Dally

archeological site in the area, is named for him. Many photographs at the Yale and District Historical Society were also donated by Milliken. In the following anecdote, he describes how the news of gold in the region broke in San Francisco.

. . .

CD2, TRACK 4

MILLIKEN: Gold was discovered in the Fraser in 1858. And the gold was first discovered on Hills Bar, which is a mile and a half south of Yale and was discovered by a party of Americans from San Francisco. One of the party being a man by the name of L.T. Hill and the one who panned the first pan, and consequently the bar was named after him. It might be interesting to note just exactly what brought out or brought on this search for gold in this portion of the river.

The Hudson's Bay Company, of course, in those days did a lot of business with San Francisco, and they had the steamer, *Beaver,* which they used to run back and forth from Victoria to San Francisco. And they went down to San Francisco, one of the usual trips, but on this particular trip they took eight hundred ounces of gold to the San Francisco mint and sold it.

And in those days, you know, there were these volunteer fire brigades, and the volunteer firemen, they used to go and sit there at night and wait for, hope for a fire, I guess, and chew the fat and smoke cigars. Well, one of these chaps, he worked in the mint. And this night when he went down to the firehall, he was telling the boys about the Hudson's Bay Company's boat being in and delivering eight hundred ounces of gold.

So they got to thinking that if the Hudson's Bay Company delivered eight hundred ounces of gold, and they knew that the boat ran from Victoria and Langley, and Langley being on the Fraser, that it must be there. So they formed a company to go and have a look, and among the company was this man, Hill.

Apparently they arrived, they took the steamer to Watkin, which is now Bellingham, and from there they, at Bellingham, they got a canoe of some type. I'd imagine a big Indian canoe, and they made their way up to, up the coast and up the Fraser. They had apparently stopped at Langley and made inquiries from the Hudson's Bay factor there, and got no information at all. As a matter of fact he said that the Hudson's Bay factor would volunteer no information about the upper country whatsoever. So they proceeded on.

And they happened to stop, they arrived at this Hills Bar, this bar we now call Hills Bar, they arrived at lunchtime. So while they were having lunch, this man, Hill, just got out the pan and tried it, and there was gold and lots of it. So you might say gold was discovered at lunchtime. And Hills Bar was the richest bar on the river.

And all the claims were actually fabulously rich. And one of the stories I heard a good many years ago was a fellow that had his claim, and he'd worked it for a little while and was ready to go south again. He'd made his fortune. He was on his way.

Panning for gold along Hills Bar. Photo: HP042629

While he was in town having a few drinks before he would get the sternwheeler to go down the river, he met a chap who was interested in buying a claim. So he said, "Yes, I've got a claim," he said. "I'll sell it to you. I'll sell it to you cheap."

So he sold him this claim for two or three hundred dollars. The fellow got the title to the claim and away he went. This fellow, he stayed around town for a few days, spending his money and having some fun, and a couple days later he saw this fellow on the street. The chap looked as though he was kind of mad at him.

He thought, "That's funny! Gee, I did that fellow a favour. I sold him that claim. It was a darn good claim, and cheap."

So he thought he'd go over and see him. And he said to the fellow, he said, "What's the matter? You appear mad."

"Well," he said, "I am! You cheated me!"

Well, he says, "I didn't! I sold you a good claim." He said, "That was one of the best claims in the bar."

"Good claim, be damned!" he said. "That thing's half gravel."

Of course, he expected it to be all gold, I guess.

There's No Sound... There's Nothing!

BILL LACHANCE

the Sole Survivor of the 1910 Glacier Snowslide

(RECORDED SEPTEMBER 3, 1965)

THE CANADIAN Pacific Railway line over Rogers Pass was one of the toughest sections of railroad in North America. The pass has an elevation of 4,534 feet (1,382 metres), runs through the Selkirk Mountains in the heart of Glacier National Park and accumulates an average of fifteen metres of snow per year. Because the mountains in that area are so steep, avalanches (or "snowslides," as Bill LaChance calls them) are common.

To protect the rail lines and allow trains to get through the pass in winter in LaChance's time, thirty-one snowsheds were built—a tremendous project that used nearly five million metres of lumber. In addition, to clear the lines not covered by snowsheds, crews used rotary plows: essentially engines powered by a steam boiler and fitted with a large cutting wheel and blower mounted to the front to cut through the snow. However, for train crews, snowslides were a reality of the job: between 1885 when the railway over Rogers Pass was completed until 1916 when it was abandoned, more than two hundred men were killed in slides. The Connaught Tunnel, completed in 1916, is eight kilometres long and was, at the time, the longest tunnel in North America; it was designed to avoid the danger and inconvenience of train stoppages that snowslides caused.

Jack of all trades E. William "Bill" LaChance (b. 1887) came west from Ontario in 1907 to work on a ranch in Manitoba, before making his way to British Columbia to work in a logging camp in 1909. Eventually he got a job working for the railroad at Revelstoke, where he was hired to

FACING: *A rotary plow used to clear rail lines, as Bill LaChance was doing when the 1910 Glacier Snowslide hit.*
Photo: HP059121

repair engines that would come from all over western Canada for service. LaChance was stationed at Rogers Pass to help engines through the pass.

LaChance's story begins on March 4, 1910, when a large snowslide covered the tracks at the base of Avalanche Mountain. LaChance was among the crew that was called to clear the line with a rotary plow. They were joined by a crew of labourers to clear rock and timber from the debris. Sometime after eleven o'clock at night, a second slide came down and buried all sixty-three men and the engine in a split second. LaChance was the sole survivor of that second slide. It was the worst slide to hit the CPR in British Columbia and contributed to the decision to abandon the route over the pass in favour of the Connaught Tunnel.

. . .

CD2, TRACK 5

ORCHARD: What were you doing on the railroad?

LACHANCE: I was in engine service. They come along and call me to go out on my engine. My engine was ready to go out and take a train up, assist a train up the hill. And we went down to the roundhouse to book out, they told us that is changed. There's slides down, and the trains that are on there, up there, are tied up. And you people, you people have got to take, that is, this engine has got to take the snowplow and go out and clear out them snowslides.

So we hitched on to the snowplow, or a rotary plow, a rotary, and away we went up the hill, you know. And we passed the passenger train at Glacier. Well that was four miles [six kilometres] up, farther up that the slide was, and we had an order from the dispatcher say that there would be no trains go past Glacier until we came back.

There was, oh, fifty-five men [sic] or so, and we went up there and we bucked right into the snowslide, you know. It had run down from the eastern side that run down and filled the cut. Oh well, I'd say maybe fourteen feet [four metres] high, fourteen feet in the cut, you see. And that had just smoothed right over, but it was a messy place because it was full of timber. This slide that come down brought timber and everything with it, everything. It cleaned the hill right off, you know. And it run, it must have run for over a mile down the hill.

And so we went in there. We were working away, and every little while we'd push in, you know, and the rotary would clean it out and then they'd come to logs and stuff like that. So then we'd back up, and all these men there with their shovels, they'd jumped down in that hole, you see, that we made, that tunnel in there. They'd jump down there and pull out this timber because the timber would break the blades off of the rotary.

Anyway, we were going to have our lunch because it was long about eleven o'clock at night, on the fourth of March, 1910, you see.

And so, anyway, I said to the engineer, "Well I'll put in a fire and then we'll have our lunch."

We had our lunch, you know, we always had lunch on the engine, and he stood up there, you know, his window was like on there, you see, and mine was over here, and he stood up there and waited 'til I put in a fire. And I had a big fire—we had a big boiler there and she had two fire doors on her, but, well you always fired through one. But then as we were just standing there I opened the two doors, and I leaned over. I leaned over like that, and got a shovel full of coal, and just as I brought my eyes back, the flame come out of that fire of those two doors, just a regular big flame, my goodness.

Of course, it was—time was going fast, you know, and I couldn't think why it had—was the boiler…? You know, sometimes perhaps a flue or something would burst and it would blow steam all out, but this was just flame that come out and no noise to it, you see.

Of course, it was only a fraction of a second. The snow come in through across the gangway, you see, and I was right there. And, well, it hit me and how, it took me right out of the gangway and up through that, to the top of that tunnel we had made. The snow was just like that up there, you see. And it picked me up and took me up there, just as this flame come out of the firebox. Well, I couldn't think what it was, but when it took me out of the engine, the snow come over the top of the engine. And it hit me in the face and, oh, I knew it was a snowslide right then, I knew what it was. I'd seen lots of them. I'd been in them before—little ones.

So as soon as the snow hit my face, you see, I just covered my face with my two hands, you see, because I knew I was in a snowslide, you see. Well then the snow, the snow got a hold of me, and what it didn't do to me was nothing. It had done everything. It pulled me out, twice my length, I guess, the way it felt. And then it just doubled me all up and rolled me like that, and I was trying to keep rolled up, you see, in a ball to go with the snow. I realized all this. I worked fast that time, and it caught this leg. It just turned it around like that and it rolled up me up and stretched me out and doubled me up and then the pressure come on. Oh, just like if there were tons on top of me. Now all the time I'm in that, I don't get one breath because the snow was got packed right tight to my face, and then this pressure come on and things kind of, kind of stopped. And it just started and it seemed like as if I was, if it was boiling, like as if it was boiling and it just, and it brought me up out of that heavy pressure.

Well, I was, when I threw my hands out I had about a, oh I had I supposed a foot of snow on top of my face. And I threw my hands out. Why, I had fresh air there, you see. Now it's just about like that shape down in the snow, you see. And I dug myself out. I thought this leg was broken, my right leg, at the knee, you see. And I thought that leg was broken, but I was going to try it anyway and get up and get back to the boiler and see if I could dig out the engineer, you see. I could realize that he was going to get hit right in the back and he was going to get knocked down against the fire, you see. And that's where he was too. He got knocked down there and he got his hands in front of him but it crushed him up against the firebox and burnt his hands some, you see.

Well, it must have been, all happened pretty fast for the engine because, after I got out, I couldn't hear the engine: the engine should have been blowing a lot of steam but there was no sound there. Everything was just dead. That's all. Everything was just dead. And there I was, and I'd lost my hat. My gloves were full of snow, were just little fine gloves, you know, for shovelling. And I threw, took them off, threw them away. And my hair was all wet. And I started, my mouth was full of blood, you see. And I spit on the snow, and there was a great big dark spot on the snow, you know. And I licked my lips and I spit again. There's another big spot of blood, and I thought I'm well off coming up now. I thought, you know, I've been hurt inside and I was afraid to put my hands inside of my overalls for fear I'd find my guts laying there, to tell the truth. That's just the way I felt now.

An engine boiler room, ca. 1910s. Photo: HP043014/Bullen and Lamb

    Well, I, at first, it, I wasn't so bad. I got out of the snow, pulled myself out of the snow and I got up and I stood up on this, my left leg, you see. I got up and I stood on that and I thought I'd drag this other one up, and I thought, well, I'll try it and I'll try and get back, you see, to where that engine is and maybe I'll save the engineer. And I just touched the toe of that foot to the snow, and the snow was soft too, and it just turned and that knee went right plump down into the snow sideways.

And, well, that was that. So, I took it and I put the right leg over the left leg, like this. And I tried to work myself back up to where it was, you see, pushing with my hands. And so it was kind of level there, so I was making headway, but when I came to where it was steeper, well, I was just pushing snow down, I wasn't going up.

So I begin to figure out—everybody's gone. If there was anybody there they'd holler the same as I did, you see. And this was all out there in front of me, you see, and there wasn't a sign of life on any of it, you see. It was, you could see, you know, on the snow. So I figured out, why, I had the, I had the order in my pocket. The engineer had passed it to me after he read it, that there would be no train go, come up the hill until we went back to the Glacier.

Well, I thought, here it is about eleven o'clock at night and it's cold, and the clothes I had on wouldn't wad a gun, you know. Well, about like this with a pair of overalls on, you see, a pair of pant overalls. And I thought it's going to be pretty cold here and I was getting kind of cold, and so I thought, everybody's gone. Everybody's passed out because anybody was in that slide never got a breath of air after they got in it. That snow was just the same as if you took and put your face down into a bag of flour and tried to breathe. That's what this snow was like.

So I thought, now there will be nobody come here 'til after daylight when they see what's going on, because they think everybody's working here and we haven't went back. But as it happened, Johnny Anderson, the road foreman, come down on the engine just as we backed up and he spoke to us there for, you know, sociable like, you know, and then he went out and away. See, he had all these men under him there. He was the road foreman. Then, he came back up.

Well that slide just came down as he left, you see. So I was on the snow all this time, and he came up and so I leaned there and I couldn't holler very loud anymore. I was hoarse. And I sat there and I thought, "This is it! I'll, I won't stand this cold here with no clothes on, and I won't stand it," and my left leg begin to get sore. I didn't know what, if there was anything wrong with it. I stood up on it; it was pretty good, you know.

And, however, I had to sit there and say my prayers. That's all there was to do. So, I, gosh, I see, a lamp, a, you know, a brakeman's lantern coming up along there, way right along the edge of the slide. By gosh, as soon as I seen that I hollered, and it stopped and it looked, and I hollered again. And…

"Who is it that's a-hollering?" he said. And, by gosh, it was Johnny Anderson, the road foreman.

And I said, "It's Bill LaChance!"

Oh he come up and he says, "Bill, where are they all?"

I said, "They're all gone." I said, "Man never got a breath of air after he got in that, that snow hit him." And I said, "There's nobody in sight, and I've been here quite a little while."

"Well," he said. "You know it was a dry slide." And Johnny was standing there in the slide up to halfway, pretty near up to his waist, you know, where there's loose snow. And he said, "Can I carry you off?"

"Why," I said, "you'd do well to walk off." I said, "You can't carry me with this snow and I can't… I'm no help."

"Well," he said. "I'll give you my Mackinaw coat," he said. And he took his Mackinaw coat off and give it to me to keep me warm, and away he went, you see. So, he went down, back down to this telephone shack and to tell them what had happened down at the Glacier, where the crew, where the train, well, where that dispatcher got his orders and gave his orders from there.

So, he was excited. Everybody was excited. And he couldn't make them understand what was the matter and he walked out of the shack and walked four miles [six kilometres] to the Glacier to tell them what was wrong. But, he sent, he got the cook out of one of the outfit cars and this watchman from the shack down there a mile, and he sent them up to take some blankets and put them on me in the snow so I wouldn't freeze to death.

Well they came up with the blanket: a Chinaman, a cook and this watchman. And they wanted to cover me up.

Well I said, "There's two slides come down now, and I've been in one of them." And I said, "If another slide comes down, I don't want to be rolled up in a blanket." Now I said, "You get me on that blanket and pull me out of here."

So they got me on the blanket, and I had this good arm, you see. And so I hooked that arm over the blanket and they was one on each corner of it. They pulled me and we're doing pretty good, you know, taking me off of the slide, but they come to a log, oh a spruce or a hemlock log, oh it'd be as big around as that, about a foot through. It was a big long log, and they said, "How are we going to get you over that?"

I said, "Pull me over it! I want to get off of this snow, off of the slide!"

They said, "We're going to hurt you!"

Well I said, "I know—but you, you won't kill me. Pull me over that log."

And, well, they went at it and they pulled 'til they pulled me over that log. It's a pretty rough log but, and so they pulled me off and they got me down to where the outfit cars were, off of the slide.

And by that time there was a dance in Revelstoke that night, and when the news had got down about the slide, well, they rung the fire bell, you know. They had, a man went up there and jerked the rope and rung the fire bell. They took all them boys from the dancehall, and everybody they could get. They put them on cars and they shot them up to the Glacier to get the men out of the snow.

And by the time they got me down there to the, to where the outfit cars, why these fellows had come from Revelstoke all the way up there and they started crowding around there and they picked me up and put me in an outfit car there—one of the sleeping cars. They piled blankets, blankets, you know. All these men were gone, why they just grabbed their blankets and they piled them all over me.

The day after the March 4 snowslide. The wrecked rotary plow La-Chance was in is under the snow. Photo: HP059126/Byron Harmon

And then somebody said, "There's another slide coming!" And away they all went and beat it. And they left me there and the doors on the car were wide open, and I was sleeping right there. And the blankets got so heavy and they were pulling my toes down, you see, and hurting my legs, so I pushed them all off. Well then they didn't come back, and it was got cold in there.

So, but anyway, the cook, he went and got a cup of tea and brought it to me, and the watchman, I said to him, "Look at my leg and see if it's hurt."

And he pulled up my overalls, you know.

ORCHARD: Which leg was this?

LACHANCE: My left leg. So he pulled up my overalls, you know. And he got sick, he got sick.

I said, "Is it bleeding?"

He says, "It's something awful."

I said, "Is it blood flowing out or is it shooting out like that?" I said. I wondered if an artery was cut, you see.

"Oh!" he says. "It's awful!"

Well, I thought, I don't know, I think time's up pretty good there. The bone was cut right in there in the shin and… anyway, he went away, left me there, and nobody turned up 'til daylight. Nobody come back up. They stayed away 'til daylight the next morning. And they all crowded back up around there and they got me out of this sleeping car. And they took me down and they put me in an express car to the Glacier and they had a doctor there, Doctor Hamilton.

They had him there. He come in and he took my shoulder and set it back in, put his fist under it, you know, and seen that he got that fixed up. And they couldn't do very much for that leg because it didn't have any, 'cause it didn't have much bandages.

Somebody said, "What will ya have? Would you have a drink of brandy?" he said. "Or would you have a cup of tea?"

Well I said, "I'll have a drink of brandy." So they brought me in a cup of tea.

Well that part of it, now I'm all ready to go to town, you see. So they takes a rotary and the superintendent's car and they put the rotary out ahead so if any slides come down, why, they clean them out as they went down to Revelstoke, you see. But they also sent a message down, over the wire, that Bill LaChance was the only man that was alive and they didn't expect him to live 'til he got to Revelstoke. I don't know why. Well that just went, you know, like every other thing.

So, my poor leg, took that, took near a year 'fore it got better, not really better, you know, that I could walk as far… After three or four months, why, I could walk all right as long as I kept it stiff, you see. But if I put any weight on it, when my knee was bent a little it'd go right down. But it come all right.

. . .

SIXTY-THREE men in total were killed on the night of March 4. LaChance describes the night as being clear with no moon and no snowfall. The men in the trench were found suspended in time: one was found rolling a cigarette and another was holding a torch, and they all looked as if they were asleep, "still with rosy cheeks." Four more bodies of Japanese labourers were found in May when the snow thawed. LaChance claimed that unlike other slides he had seen, this slide made no noise. The road foreman, Johnny Anderson, lost his brother—who was also a foreman—in that slide, along with four other foremen.

By noon the next day (March 5), LaChance was in the hospital in Revelstoke, where he spent the next several months, and all of the schoolchildren came and crowded around him to see the survivor of the slide. In the end, his left leg was badly cut, his right leg was broken and twisted near the knee, and he had several broken ribs—though he did not know it for several months because he was lying down. His right leg was so swollen for a while that amputation was considered. After his rehabilitation, LaChance took a job as a CPR engineer from Vancouver to the B.C.–Alberta border at Field for six years. He then moved to the coast, where he worked as a steam engineer in the forest industry.

Paid by the Skin

MAX LOHBRUNNER

on the Seal-hunting Life

(RECORDING DATE UNKNOWN)

ALTHOUGH SEAL hunting is a controversial issue today, Canada's Aboriginals have hunted seals for more than four thousand years. Among the Inuit, seal meat is prized as a rich source of iron and vitamins, and the pelts are used to make warm clothing. In non-Native communities, seal pelts were also valued for their warmth, and seal oil was used as fuel for oil lamps, as an ingredient in soap and as a lubricant.

Commercial seal hunting began in Europe in 1515 and became a very profitable industry. In Victoria, the commercial industry began in 1869, and by the first decade of the 1900s, there were 122 sealing schooners based out of that city. When commercial seal hunting was at its peak, many Native people owned their own boats and hired white people as navigators. However, the North Pacific Fur Seal Convention of 1911, which addressed wildlife conservation, introduced rules to preserve and protect the seal populations. This treaty put a halt to the sealing industry in Victoria. Today, Canada is one of just five countries in the world that engages in commercial seal hunting.

Max Lohbrunner (1887–1973) came to Victoria from New York in 1887, when he was 6 months old, with his father, who was a carpenter. As a child, he fished for halibut, crabs and shrimp in Victoria harbour, and as a young adult hunted seals. The following anecdote offers in-depth details about

ABOVE: *Life aboard a sealing ship, 1890s.*
Photo: HP028032

the lifestyle of sealers and of life aboard ships. Lohbrunner describes competition among individuals, yet camaraderie and teamwork as well.

. . .

LOHBRUNNER: They first started to seal out of Victoria in 1869. I didn't show up until 1887. But, from the time I could row a boat or paddle a boat, I was on the water, fishing out of Victoria. And I hunted here as well, as a kid, for market, them days there. Game. Everything was wide open.

Then I started to hunt seal, on the schooners in 1903, on my first vessel that I signed on, a schooner called the *Diana*. She was a white schooner, and it was a one-year trip. I was 14 or 15 at the time. That included the Oregon coast, California. When I say the coast, we generally sailed outside of a hundred miles [160 kilometres]—from that off maybe to five hundred [eight hundred kilometres]—wherever we could find seal.

Back again up along the coast, along the British Columbia coast, Queen Charlottes, up along the Alaskan coast, up around Kodiak, towards the Aleutian Islands, all along the Aleutian Islands. Sometimes I crossed over the Japan coast, the Copper Islands on the Russian side, back into the Okhotsk Sea and outside the Japan coast, down to the southern part of the Çorlu Islands, then back into the Bering Sea, leaving the Bering Sea again in the later part of October, November to make the run home to Victoria.

And an Indian schooner, what we called an Indian schooner, they had a white captain, a white mate, probably a white second mate, and the rest were Indian canoes. Two men in a canoe. Sometimes an Indian, he got paid so much a skin. And if there were two Indians, that was split in half between the two of them. But was very often the case, the Indians would have their wives along, and some of the women could handle a canoe as good as the men—sometimes better. And it meant that all that money was split up between the two in the family. Where if there were two separate Indians, that went to two different families. And there's a lot of them in their high boats, some of the Indians that were high boats, some of them there had women who sealed for a number of years and they could handle a canoe and sail a canoe in all kinds of weather, sometimes better than their husbands. Because that was their business in the stern, and attending to the sail all those times.

The average white boat would be in the neighborhood from eighteen to twenty-one feet [five and a half to six and a half metres]. Mostly twenty feet. An Indian canoe could be anywhere from eighteen feet to sometimes twenty-three and twenty-four feet [five to around seven metres]. Sometimes, in some of the larger vessels, they would pack probably eighteen to twenty-four canoes according to the size of the vessel, as many as they could put aboard on both sides.

Well, if the weather was fine, and if we'd seen seal around the day before or that evening, the boats were out sometimes before daylight. Just at the break of day, you put the boats over the side. The idea would be for the each boat to keep as far apart as they could. And as they were sailing, the lead boat still going off further. If you went to winter [south of, or below] to a seal that was sleeping, he'd wake up every time. If you were a mile from him, he'd smell you and wake up. And the idea was that the lead boat was always way ahead of the rest of the boats. And the next second lead boat, he was so far astern to him so that a sleeping seal wouldn't wake up. In other words there, one boat would be behind the other all the way, from the lead boat to the windward boat, and sometimes that spread would be half a mile, so as to give each boat a berth without a seal to smell them. Supposing I happen to see a seal, and I happened to be, we'll say, in the middle—boats to winter and boats to nord [north of, or above] of me. As soon as I seen that seal, if he was to winter to me, I'd sail along until I got to nord of him. I'd drop my sail. And when I'd done that, the other boat to winter to me, he was watching me all the time, he'd slack away a sheet, so he wouldn't get to winter of that seal, so he wouldn't wake up.

Then I'd drop my sail, and then I'd use my oars, and I'd sneak up on him. And when I'd get so close, I'd turn around to the boat puller and tap him on the shoulders; he'd take his oars in. Sometimes maybe within fifty or a hundred yards [forty-five to ninety metres]. If it was heavy weather I'd try to sail within ten, fifteen yards [nine or ten metres] of him. And

I'd tap him on his shoulder; he'd slide his oars in very easy so he wouldn't make a noise or touch the boat to wake the seal. And the boat steerer in the meantime, he's holding against the oars, holding against the wind and sea, and it was blowing hard. The boat was really drifting away from the wind and sea. But that seal was also moving. He's laying on his side with his hind flipper and his front flipper curled, in that fashion, like a jug. And he's got his head to lowered, and that head is always swinging. Sometimes he sleeps with his head underwater but when he takes a breath, he raises the half his head and he just takes a breath and he drops his head again underwater.

Seal pelts on the deck of a sealing ship, 1890s. Photo: HP093313

Well then, when you get abreast of him, you keep a little off to one side. You watch which side the back of his head was on. You try to take a shot. You don't shoot him in the jaw, you can break the jaw all up and he'd still be life in him. But if you got a good shot in the hap, hap his head, or the back of the head, he was easily killed, if it was only one or two buckshot.

And anyways, after you got up so close, you'd motion to the boat steerer with your arm, either right or left, that you wanted to go on this side of him. He wouldn't be going straight for the seal, he'd go a little bit parallel with him. So that I got a better chance to shoot diagonal, sideways to the back of the head. But if the seal was restless and he looked up, and he made a splash, then it was the case of chase him, chase him with

The Northwest Coast pelagic seal fishing fleet in Victoria Harbour, 1901.
Photo: HP033220

the oars. Which wasn't always so good. If you could get him sleeping, you saved a lot of time; you were holding the other boats up too, if you had to chase him.

If it happened to be blowing hard, sometimes we're glad to get one or two or three round seal without being skinned, in the boat for ballast. Makes a boat a whole lot stiffer, because you're sailing nearly all the time, you only use your oars when you're chasing the seal or working on him. But you keep two or three or even four seal if was blowing real hard for ballast, means a lot to ya. And there's other times when the weather's fine, if you got a spare minute, after you get two or three seal you're using the oars practically. Without any sail, if there was no wind at all, and there's that much extra weight, and the boat down that much further in the water for you to push and to pull and to maneuver. You turn around then, it's two pieces of wood laid across the boat with canvas in the middle. And it's something like a stretcher you might say. You can slip, slip these two pieces of wood, bars through the openings on the side, and you lay that across. And when you're skinning, all the blood and grease half the time there from the carcass is in that. And when you take the hide off, you just dip it, and then you throw it back under the boat-puller seat. And you slide the carcass over the side. You don't keep that greasy carcass. But all the time you're skinning it. While you're skinning, as well, they're keeping a lookout, and you're still skinning and watching in between times as well, to see if you can see anything. They're always on the lookout.

A hunter, he was paid by the skin. We had, from the time I started, what we had, what we called a sliding scale. The first seal that a hunter got, I'm speaking now back in 1903, the first seal we got, we got two dollars and half a skin for him. That's the hunter. The boat puller and the boat steerer, he get fifty cents a piece, for every seal I killed. But he had ten dollars a month of wages. And that was big money them days.

For every seal that I killed, up to fifty, I had two dollars and a half. But as soon as I got fifty seal, I got three dollars. Not for that fifty-first seal, but right from the start. That's the reason why there was so many hunters were lost and drownded [sic], "rustling" as we called it, staying out in heavy weather. Take a chance to try to make over the fifty or over a hundred. Well, from fifty-one skins on, we had three dollars. But if I broke a hundred, I had three dollars and half a skin, right from the very start. And if I broke a hundred and fifty, I had four dollars a skin. But if I made two hundred, I got four and a half dollars a skin, right from the very start. But as a rule, it was pretty hard them days to make two hundred skins.

But the ones that did, they had that money right from the start. Others were within two or three skins, of that amount. And there was times it was still blowing, there was no seal around but he'd hang on under double reefs before he'd go aboard. He hadn't made his two hundred. We were late in the Bering Sea, we were probably thinking this might be our last lowering, the weather's been that tough, you see, we're on the verge, we figured the next breeze we're gonna put the mainsail on her to head her for Victoria. And it be a case then sometimes there that he'd stay out there right up 'til dark. He was probably lucky enough to get that one or two that he needed.

And there's other times he had to come home without it. But it's very often the case, sometimes he had a good hunter friend and he'd already made his two hundred. And before the day was over, if the weather conditions got that bad that he, that there was no chance, and all the rest of the boats were gone. Sometimes you'd probably get in touch with him, give him a signal with the oar you're gonna speak him. He'd sail down to ya, and if you had a couple of spares, you'd toss them over to him, for him to make that extra two hundred. Which he probably only needed two or three. But, there was the case when the skipper wasn't even supposed to know anything about this. You had to keep this under your hat.

Sometimes is the case, they were all sports, and was not very often the case, the skipper would close his eyes to what was going on but it wasn't entered. But, it would amount to any quantity like that was never done unless was done on the quiet. But as a rule, the majority of the boats were pretty close together. It was very often the case among friends sometimes, one would slip the low boat a skin or two and the other fella would probably do the same thing to try to help him out, try to make that two hundred. But, it was very often the case where there was nobody had two hundred, among all the boats. That was the reason why there was so many sealers lost "rustling" as they called it. And I've seen times there, all the boats have been aboard, but there'd be a few scattered seal around, and they'd be hanging on to try and break that fifty, or to break that hundred. Because it all meant a whole lot at the end of the, end of the season.

. . .

LOHBRUNNER claims that when the sealing industry closed in Victoria in 1911, it was supposed to be for a fifteen-year interval and that the government was supposed to compensate the sealers for the loss of their

The sealing schooner Diana, *the first vessel Max Lohbrunner signed on to, ready for sea, ca. 1900s. Photo: HP099724/Ben Williams Leeson*

industry. The Japanese government paid all of the Japanese sealers who worked out of Victoria, and all of the non-Japanese men who worked on Japanese boats, within six months. However, Lohbrunner claims that the Canadian government still had not paid the Victoria sealers up to the date of this interview in the 1960s. He says that he is the last of the "old hunters" left, and that he would like to go back to sealing when the treaty expires.

Lohbrunner was still working on helping the families of the sealers obtain the millions of dollars (with the interest accumulated on the funds back to 1911) that he claims is owed to them. Lohbrunner owned a house in Victoria with his wife, and lived in his boat on the wharf in Victoria built by the sealers in 1905, and was the only person in the 1960s permitted to do so.

(5)

Pioneering Women

THE EXPERIENCE of women in pre-war British Columbia was vastly different from that of men. Just as Orchard interviewed Aboriginals to allow them to cast themselves as active participants in his narrative, so he also asked women to tell their stories. As such, his recordings give us some understanding of what life was like for women at that time.

Many women came into communities that men had established and that men worked in, and therefore found themselves in predominantly male environments. In fact, from 1870 right through to 1911, males in British Columbia outnumbered females 2:1 (coincidentally, the same ratio reflected in the interviews in the entire Orchard Collection). These numbers were skewed somewhat, however, as women lived mostly in the

FACING: *Mrs. James Douglas, née Amelia Connelly, 1865.*
Photo: HP008228

cities, meaning that men comprised as much as 70 to 75 per cent of the population in more remote locales.

Regardless of where in the province they were located, women were not allocated the same rights as men. For example, women were not given the right to vote in British Columbia until 1917. Even though, politically, women were second-class citizens, they considered themselves highly motivated, active participants in the community. As their anecdotes reveal, some of these first-generation female immigrants adapted easily to the new landscapes and culture, whereas others did not and were quite miserable.

Cried Every Day for a Year

MRS. H. WILLIAMS

on Making a New Home

(RECORDED NOVEMBER 5, 1964)

MRS. H. WILLIAMS (b. 1895) is just one of countless women who came to British Columbia and initially hated it. (It is somewhat telling that we do not have her first name. At the time, many women's identities were subsumed by their husbands: her initial, H, and her last name, Williams, are those of her husband, Harry Williams.) Many women must have felt the same homesickness that Williams communicates; and while it is true that many men would also have been missing home, most married women who came to B.C. at the time were following their husbands, who had come by choice.

Williams was born in Dunfermline, Scotland, and was married there on February 24, 1914, before honeymooning in Glasgow for a week. The anecdote she shares begins after this week. Mr. Williams worked as a carpenter when they first moved to Wilmer, in the Columbia Valley in eastern British Columbia, making flumes for a water system out in the bush. At the time Williams describes, the area was booming with ore mining.

. . .

WILLIAMS: We sailed from Glasgow on the seventh of March, 1914. And I think we were fifteen days on the water and then we came into St. John's. And then we took the train from St. John's to Montreal and we stayed there a whole day. And then we got the train, and we were

CD3, TRACK 1

ABOVE: *The Windsor Hotel in Athalmer, ca. 1910.*
Photo: HP060236

four—four days or five days on the train coming across the continent. Then we came off at Golden, and we went to the hotel there and we stayed there for two weeks.

And then we started up for the valley. And then we took the bus home. No it's not the bus, the democrat [a horse-drawn wagon], with a family the name of Macintosh from Spillimacheen up to Athalmer, which was quite a few miles. And I was scared to death on that democrat because there were two men there I didn't like the look of, but my husband guaranteed they were all right.

Well I said, "I don't know." I was scared of Indians, scared to this day. And we came right along at the bottom of the Rockies. I'll never forget it. On the old wagon road, you know it wasn't a—wasn't a good road at all. And I'll never forget coming into Athalmer at twelve o'clock at night.

Well then, I went upstairs and had a room there. But, oh, I thought, all wooden buildings, you know, and we have stone buildings at home. They're maybe not just so comfortable either. But, oh, I was very cold there and I began to cry in the morning. Oh, I didn't like it.

And my husband took hold of me and he said, "Oh you'll get used to this."

I said, "I don't like it."

He said, "Come and look at the lake." He said, "I'm sure it'll be like a Loch Lomond."

And I did look out and I said, "That's not like Loch Lomond." "Oh," I said, "I don't want to stay here."

Well, in the morning, he hired the, the Joe Davis, you would know him. He had a wooden leg, I think, but he had a most beautiful team, a black team. So he hired him to take us up to Wilmer.

So going up to Wilmer he said, "You think you'll like this place?"

Well, I said, "It's much better looking than that place down there. I didn't like that at all."

Well he said, you know, oh, he said, "It's not like home."

I said, "No, no. Not like home at all."

However, went up to Wilmer, and went into the hotel there. And, you know, I rather liked that place. But Wilmer was a very busy place then, a lot of mines. Oh, it was busy! And everything there nearly, you know, hotels and a shoemaker shop. Oh, I just couldn't settle down to that; however, made the most of it.

Well went out to the ranch on the first of July, and we got Mr. Manson to take our belongings out. You know, we had to buy furniture and beds and mattresses, and so on. Went out to the ranch, which was seven miles [eleven kilometres] out from Wilmer, right in amongst the sticks, you know. I thought, well I'll have to make the most of it anyway. So, went up there and, oh dear, built. The house was built in ten days, ten days. The glass had to be sent for, for the windows, the panes, windowpanes. And that had to come from Golden by boat. So we just had to wait on, and that's just what I was—I just got so nervous there you know.

And then the coyotes started too. Oh my husband always sound asleep, you know. Oh I heard this coyote, and I jumped out of bed and I shook him. I said, "Harry, waken." I said, "There's an, there's an awful noise here."

He, he said, "A noise? What is it like?"

I said, "It sounds like a woman crying." And I had no sooner said that than this coyote put out another yell.

And he said, "Oh," he said, "that's a coyote."

I said, "What's a coyote?"

He says, "An animal like a dog."

I said, "I'm going home to Scotland tomorrow. I'm going back to Scotland."

"No, no," he said, to quote him, "No, no." He said, "You'll be all right here after a while."

I said, "Oh, I don't like this place."

Well the family that he came out to work for was, um, he was married. Mr. Foster was married, and he'd a wife and two children then. Or one child, I think. And Mrs. Foster's mother lived with them. So and then they had a, a maid for their children and to do the housework. So she and I got very, very well acquainted, and we used to go down the lane for a walk. Oh it was a pretty place too—pretty. It had its beauty spots, you know. And she came from England and I came from Scotland. And we would sit on the fence and we'd cry until we couldn't see each other. Awfully sorry that ever we'd come out to Canada.

Athalmer in 1913, located beside the town of Wilmer. Photo: HP036293

My husband would come home for his supper and he'd say—we, we got the electric light in that little shack. That was the only thing I was sorry to leave, you know. And he said, "Well, have you been crying today again?"

I said, "No." Not an awful lie, you know. I said, "No."

"Yes," he said, "you have." He said, "You know, if I knew anyone going home to Scotland, I would let you go home for two years. For this must be terrible on you."

"Oh well," I said, "I'll maybe get used to it." But, you know, right to this day I like Scotland better than Canada. It was such a change. Going from Dunfermline over to Edinburgh to the pantomimes. And oh my, those lovely halls—never forget it. However, I got used to it. And then the coyote, I got used to that too.

PIONEERING WOMEN 121

And then there was one day I was dressing by the heater in the—in the sitting room. My husband always gave me my breakfast in bed. And then he started up the fires, you know. And I was dressing by the heater, and here I saw something coming towards me, coming across the carpet on the sitting room. It was a water lizard. It looked like he was swimming but there was no water. It was on the carpet he was doing this, you know. Well I just looked and I didn't know what to do or—woulda run out of the house. I couldn't do that, for I wasn't dressed. And my husband had started a good fire in the heater. Not in the heater, in the cookstove in the kitchen. And it was just the room adjoining. I thought, oh dear, what am I going to do? So I just got the dustpan and I put the dustpan down and it crawled up and I just lifted the lid off the stove and—[laughter]. Oh dear. I didn't know what it was until my husband told me.

A home in Wilmer, ca. 1910. Photo: HP017887

So I went out to meet him coming from his work at twelve o'clock for his lunch. Oh he could see I had got an awful fright.

He said, "Well, what's wrong?"

I said, "You know there was a crocodile in the house today?"

"A crocodile?" he said, "Where do you think that came from?"

I says, "I don't know but I'm not going back into that house!"

"Oh yes," he said, "You will, come on with me." So he took hold of me, went back. And he said, "Well, what did you do with that eh—"—he knew it was a water lizard you know—"What did you do with that animal?"

"Well," I said, "I'm sorry that I have to tell ye, I lifted the stove and I, the lid off the stove, the cookstove, and I put it in there."

"Oh," he said, "did it make a noise?"

I said, "Yes, it cracked and cracked and crickled and—" But I said, "It's safe."

"Oh," he said, "that's terrible."

Well I said, "I couldn't come for you. I couldn't run up to the ranch after you."

"No," he said.

Well that's, that's my life, you know.

Oh dear me, and I used to write to my mother every week. And she would always ask me—I used to get a letter from her every week too—always ask me if I was homesick. But I'd never answer that, no. I didn't want her to worry. No use.

So when I went home in 1920, oh I had my daughter then, she was four years old. It wasn't so bad after she was born, you know, but I went home for a trip to Scotland. Stayed all winter. So my mother said to me—I stayed with my mother, you know—my mother said, "Well, have you been homesick?" She said, "I've asked you in all the letters but you've never answered."

I said, "Homesick, Mother, I'll tell you now since we're face to face." But I said, "I cried every day for a whole year."

Well she started to cry, too. She said, "And you never told me."

I said, "There was no use, there was no use." But, oh I just got over it, you know. Oh dear me.

. . .

MRS. WILLIAMS'S husband, Harry, died in 1955, and she flew to Scotland to visit her twin sister who begged her to move back. However, Williams says, "If my family wasn't here, I would go. It's nice there, and it's home." Williams also claims that she was very happy in Wilmer after she got settled there and got used to the life. She claims that the transition from city life to the lifestyle in Wilmer was the hardest part of the homesickness.

Monarch of All I Survey

SARAH GLASSEY

*the First Woman to
Pre-empt Land in British Columbia*

(RECORDED JUNE 28, 1961)

THE EXPERIENCE of Sarah Glassey (1881–1962) as a newcomer to British Columbia stands in stark contrast to that of Mrs. Williams. When she settled in the Kispiox Valley, Glassey was the first single woman to first pre-empt and then own land in British Columbia in almost forty years. She loved her life there. Glassey details her experience, and in doing so reveals many attitudes of men toward women at that time.

Sarah Glassey is a very important figure in British Columbia history, yet other than in the Orchard Collection and in this book, she remains unknown. Truly, the story of Sarah Glassey illustrates exactly why oral history collections such as Orchard's are so important: heroes exist among everyday people, not just among our leaders.

Glassey first came to northern British Columbia from Spokane, Washington, at the end of April 1906 to visit her sister and brother-in-law who owned land thirty-two kilometres from Hazelton on the telegraph line. When she arrived, they sent the policeman and his wife to meet and house her because, according to Glassey, "in the early days it wasn't considered proper for a single girl to stay at the hotels." She left three months later, in August, not thinking she would ever be back, since Hazelton and the people there seemed to her to be "wild and woolly!"

Glassey did return in 1910 to visit her sister, and her second trip was entirely different from the first. Of the sixty people aboard the boat she sailed in on, she was the only woman. Work on the Grand Trunk Pacific

FACING: *Sarah Glassey carried a rifle and bagged
more birds than any man in the Kispiox valley! In this photo,
Miss L. Ford takes aim, 1900. Photo:* HP098878

railroad had brought a rush of construction workers to the area, and she noted that Hazelton was booming with new roads being built throughout the Kispiox Valley. She felt like she fell in love with the country during that visit.

On February 4, 1859, Governor James Douglas had passed British Columbia's first pre-emption act, which gave settlers the right to purchase public land for ten shillings per acre. In 1872, Canada passed the Dominion Lands Act to encourage settlement in the prairies. The act gave homesteaders the right to acquire 160 acres [sixty-five hectares] of land for free (well, free except for the payment of a small administration fee) as long as they promised to cultivate at least forty acres [sixteen hectares] of that land over the next three years. During that time, settlers remained tenants on the property; however, if they could show "improvement" of their land, they could eventually own it. Initially, purchasing land was open to anyone, and at least two women pre-empted land in 1873, but the next year the law was amended to exclude women (unless widowed). It was not until 1911 that women were given the same right as men to pre-empt land. The act came to an end in 1918.

In this anecdote, Glassey describes moving up north and pre-empting land outside of Hazelton in 1911. After her marriage to Bert Glassey in Hazelton three years later, Glassey sold her land to a German man who also bought the two parcels of land owned by Norwegian settlers on either side of hers to raise cattle. She notes that the German man initially would not "do business" with her, but only with her husband. Finally, he gave in and dealt with her directly.

. . .

CD3, TRACK 2

GLASSEY: My sister and brother-in-law tried to persuade me to live with them, and I said, "Oh no." I didn't think that I should do that, because two women couldn't live in the same house and get along for any length of time. And I said I didn't think that we could either, any more than any other two women.

And so my brother-in-law said, "Well, I'll give you five acres [two hectares] down on the flat, there and you can build yourself a house up there."

The government office in Hazelton in 1909, where Mr. Allison granted the first pre-emption to a woman in B.C. in almost forty years. Photo: HP023232

And I said, "Well, what sense would there be in that? If I was going to come up here and live, why take five acres when I could take 160 acres [sixty-five hectares]?" You know, take up a pre-emption.

And so he said, "All right, we'll do that. We'll go out and look the country over, and you pick out where you want to, if it hasn't already been staked. We'll, you pick out where you would like a place."

So he saddled the horses, and he and I rode and went all over the country. And finally I picked out a place that I thought I would like, and we staked it. And when we went into Hazelton, when I was coming out again, we went to the government office to register this.

The government agent, who was a Mr. Allison (he was a brother-in-law of Sir Richard McBride's [noted B.C. politician]), and the clerks in

Hazelton, ca. 1910. Photo: HP001100

the office couldn't believe their ears that a woman was staking a preemption. And Mr. Allison told me that I was the first woman in British Columbia, after women got their rights, to do such a thing.

And they thought, well, we'll never see *her* again, you know—that attitude. And, but they thought they'd carry on and register me just the same, but they certainly never expected to see me again. That winter, I think I was buying every magazine that had any little houses in. I became quite an architect too, drawing up what I wanted for a house on my place, you know, and making measurements and everything.

And much to everyone's surprise, when the first boat arrived in Hazelton I was on board it. And with chickens and all my furniture and household belongings and everything. I had come to be one of them. And they just couldn't believe their eyes. And anyhow, I did, I went up there. And it took over a year before I was able to get a cabin built on my place, but I think I'm getting a little ahead of the story.

I have to tell you of our trip up *that* river, *that* particular time. We came up on the *Inlander*, I think it was, and Captain [John] Bonser, who was notorious, especially for his language, was the captain of that boat. And when we got to Kitselas Canyon, he ordered all passengers off, and especially the women. He didn't want, as he said, a damn woman left on that boat. He said women were bad luck to not only a boat, they were bad luck anyhow. And so we all got off, and I think it was two miles [three kilometres] or something like that from one side of the canyon to the other. So we all hurried up to get around there to watch the boat going through the canyon.

So we were enjoying watching. And they kept, inch by inch it was going on, and they were having to line themselves through and they were making it wonderfully well but slow. And they almost had about one more turn of the paddlewheel to go and they'd be through, when the line broke, and away went the boat down through the canyon and down and into the rocks and broke her wheel. And she was really battered up.

And he came storming downstairs, says "Oh, there must be a woman on board this boat! There *must* be a woman! Look around and check the boat!"

And there they found two women had hid in the freight because they were determined to go, have the name of having gone through that canyon.

And he said, "I knew it! I knew it! Nothing but a woman would have caused this!"

And these two women came out just looking like two whipped culprits, you know. Oh, they were so frightened. They weren't frightened of the canyon, they were frightened of the captain.

So, anyhow, there wasn't anything that could be done about it. They had stayed, and he didn't know it and no one else knew it, and we hadn't even missed them ourselves. And so they worked all that afternoon and all night to fix the boat, to repair it to go through the trip.

The next day, we had our lunch and we were all to get off. This time they were counted. The purser [likely Wiggs O'Neill, see chapter 7] had to stand at the gangplank and count us as we came off, just like so many sheep coming off. I think the two women were quite relieved to be able to get off, too, with a whole skin, you know, because the captain was noted to have a pretty bad temper and they didn't know what he was going to do to them.

So, anyhow, this time they *did* go through the canyon perfectly. They came right through, and we all got on again and went on with our trip up the river.

So, as I say, I arrived in Hazelton, much to everyone's surprise, and went up to the Kispiox Valley. And it was a little over a year before I was able to have a cabin built on my pre-emption and got myself established there.

The first night I was over there—my nearest neighbour was a mile away and a river between—but, of course, when I moved over, the river was frozen over so that wasn't too bad. I could easily go walk over. But the first night I was there I was so happy, and I'd look out the window and there was the Babine Mountains in front of me, and the northern lights were flashing around. You never saw anything so beautiful.

And the coyotes were howling down on the flat and there was a shriek owl in the tree shrieking its head off, and in another tree a hoot owl. *Hoo, hoo! Hoo, hoo!*

And I thought, "Go on! Do as you like! You're not frightening me. I'm monarch of all I survey!" And I looked over and there were my 160 acres around me, and me in the middle of it, and I thought I really felt as though I was monarch of all I surveyed.

And I looked out there, and looked at the scene of the Babine Mountains and the northern lights, and you never saw anything so beautiful as those lights flashing on those mountains. And I thought to myself, "Well, anyone who couldn't believe in God needed to look at a scene like that."

And I just bowed my head in thanksgiving that I was part of that country right then. I felt as though I really belonged.

The Kispiox Valley. Photo: 14-2 E 49

So, things went on for a while and my brother-in-law said to me, he says, "Now the next thing that you have to do is to learn how to shoot."

And I said, "Shoot?" I said, "What am I going to shoot?"

And he said, "Well, you might meet a bear."

And I said, "Well, I hope I do. That is a dream of my life to meet a bear."

And I never did. I never did and I used to walk. They used to tell me that in the fall when the fish were spawning, you know, that the bears used to go along there to pick these fish out. And I would walk miles along the river edge to try and see if I could see a bear right in its natural surroundings, but I never did. I think everyone else saw a bear but me. I never did see one.

In the meantime, I'd got acquainted with my husband, and who is my husband now—he wasn't then—but I got acquainted with him, and he gave me a .22 rifle. I think that was the first present he ever gave me. I guess he thought, well, I could go and shoot myself or something. But anyhow, he gave me my rifle, so my brother-in-law taught me to shoot, and we used to go out hunting together for grouse. So he taught me how to take aim and how he could see grouse, and I couldn't see them. And anyhow, he showed me and told me how to find them and everything.

And he had a beautiful Llewellin setter, a thoroughbred, and I had my little fox terrier, and we used to take them around. And that Llewellin setter taught that little fox terrier to hunt, until it was the best bird dog in the valley, that little fox terrier was.

So anyhow, I got up at three o'clock in the morning. Of course, there's no darkness up there. It was all daylight. So three o'clock in the morning on a Sunday morning, I got up and I thought, well I'm going out hunting. So I took the little fox terrier with me, and we went out hunting. We went up the valley a mile or two, and he put up a bunch of grouse.

There must have been about fourteen in the bunch, and I got so excited at seeing them that I just stood there petrified, you know, and they flew in all directions until I, I was so bewildered I didn't see where any of them lit in the trees. And I was looking around, looking around in the trees, and finally I saw what I thought was part of a limb sticking out straight, you know, with no leaves on. And I looked and looked at that and I thought, is that a grouse or is it a limb? I'm going to shoot at it and just see what happens.

So when I took aim, I was so excited the rifle was just going around in circles, so I had to get down on my knees, and I put my elbow on one knee and took aim and shot. And the thing fell down and it was a grouse, and it had made its neck so long (they do that so you won't recognize what they are) and it fell down, and my brother-in-law had said, whenever you shoot a grouse, when you pick it up, be sure and twist its neck in case it's only wounded, you know, to finish it so it won't suffer.

And I went to pick this up to do just as he'd told me to do, and I had shot the head right off of it. Now that was an accident! It wasn't any good shooting, and I'm not bragging at all because it never happened again.

But do you know that I bagged more birds than any man in that valley? And one of the men got jealous of me because I had done that, and you know, it's not allowed now, but pre-emptors were allowed to shoot any time of the year, whether it was in season or out of season, for their table, you see.

And this man went and reported me to the government agent. The rest of the settlers up there thought that was an awful thing to do to the only woman that had had the courage to come up there. But every day, winter or summer, I either went out fishing or hunting, but I always took the gun and I always had a line and a hook in my pocket, and my pocket knife, and I used to cut a limb off of a willow tree and make my fishing rod with that, and fish my trout out of the Kispiox.

Honestly, it was the most wonderful life. I lived on that pre-emption alone, and my little dog—he finally got killed—and I lived there nearly three years. And I don't think I was ever as healthy or as happy in my life as I was when I was up there. You could go out in the woods and pick out any imaginable wild fruit. Your living didn't cost you anything as long as you had flour and sugar and butter. We usen't to buy eggs like you buy them now. They were put up in tins, you know, dry.

You have to do a certain amount of improvement on the place before you could prove up on it, you know. So I happened to announce that I was going to start in clearing land, and, of course, that nearly terrified all the men because they thought I was sure going to kill myself by falling a tree on top of myself. So one of them undertook to teach me how to fell trees.

And so he said, "You know, you take your axe and hold it up against the tree, and where if the tree is leaning this way and you put your axe that way, well, you chop this way and then it'll fall where you want it to. But if you chop this other way, it's liable to fall on you."

So he taught me how to fell a tree, and one day I chopped down seven trees and limbed them and burnt the limbs and everything, and there they were. Much to everyone's amusement when they came and I showed them what I did. I was quite proud of my efforts, but they said, well, it looked as though a beaver had been around. So that finished me, I wasn't chopping down anymore trees, which I didn't. But I…

There was an old Indian down in the Kispiox Valley that he had his fishing grounds further up in the valley, and I got him to come and clear three acres [1.2 hectares]. All you needed was three acres cleared, so he cleared three acres. And the trees that he chopped down, he made firewood for me. So I was well supplied with firewood and had all the improvement on my place. But I was told after, when the man came to inspect the work that I had done, the house alone would have been all I'd have needed because it was, at that time, the best house that was built in the valley. I had a real nice house. I brought my windows and doors up from Victoria for my house, and they were different to any that was in the country. And it was really wonderful living there, though, but going out you were so free, and there was a man about a mile [1.6 kilometres] further up the valley from me. He had quite a large ranch and he used to go out working, but he gave me permission to go help myself to any vegetables I wanted.

ORCHARD: You didn't grow your own vegetables?

GLASSEY: Oh I did, but they weren't like what his were. Mine were little bits of things, you know, because the ground wasn't as cultivated as his. He had horses that he could cultivate it. Mine was just spaded. And so, oh yes, I had a little garden that I could run down and get a few little things out of, you know. And a little fence around it so the horses wouldn't come in.

This Country Was a Dream

MYRA DEBECK

on Her Mother's Rustic Life

(RECORDED NOVEMBER 11, 1964)

MYRA KING DEBECK (1890–1979) illuminates details about childbirth, the rustic life and how women of her mother's generation would have travelled to the Okanagan Valley. DeBeck was the daughter of Sophie and Price Ellison (October 6, 1852–December 12, 1932), who was a very important politician in the Okanagan in the pre-war years.

Ellison had settled in Vernon, having come via California from England in 1876. At first he was a gold miner and blacksmith, but eventually became an exceptional farmer and orchardist. He married Sophie Johnson on December 7, 1884, and they had several children. In 1898, Ellison won his first provincial election, and over the next eighteen years he was re-elected five times, representing the constituencies of Yale and Okanagan as provincial Minister of Finance and Agriculture, and then as Chief Commissioner of Lands and Works in Premier Richard McBride's government.

Ellison's daughters, too, were leaders within the community. DeBeck, for example, was born in Vernon but educated at Havergal College in Toronto in 1906. She then went on to earn her BA in economics at McGill University in Montreal in 1911, and two years later, her MA in economics, also at McGill. She moved back to Vernon to teach physical education before marrying Howard DeBeck in 1920. The couple had two children before Howard died in 1929 at the age of just 39. In addition

ABOVE: *Many women rode long distances in an English riding habit sitting side-saddle, ca. 1890.* PHOTO: H-04871

to raising her children, Myra DeBeck was a member of the Vernon and District Women's Canadian Club, the Alpine Club of Canada, the University Women's Club and the Girl Guides of Canada, North Okanagan Division, among many other clubs. As well, she worked on many projects with her father, including his report which led to the creation of the first park in British Columbia: Strathcona Park on Vancouver Island. (In fact, she was the first woman to climb the mountains in the Vancouver Island Alps in Strathcona Park.) She died in Victoria in 1979, but is buried in the Vernon cemetery.

In the following story, DeBeck mentions the Cherry Creek gold rush. From 1863 to 1895, while other larger rushes were occurring in British Columbia, the town of Hilton (now known as Cherryville, for the wild chokecherries that grow locally on the riverbanks) housed a postal outlet and a small mining camp of approximately 100 people at any given time, half of whom would have been of Chinese origin. Cherryville is located in the northern Okanagan Valley.

. . .

DEBECK: All our family were born here, and all were born without benefit of hospital and practically all without benefit of nurse or doctor. For her very last baby, my mother had a nurse and she said it was *heavenly* to be looked after.

Once she had an Indian woman that helped her. Once she had one of the early pioneers, not as early as my parents, but a woman that I didn't know was supposed to be a midwife. But not so many years ago, the daughter of this woman said, of course, Mother was a midwife. Well, she didn't assist at the birth, I know, but she did come in and help.

At the time that Mrs. Sovereign [Myra DeBeck's sister Ellen] was born, there was a doctor at Lansdowne, but that was nineteen miles [thirty kilometres] away. And by the time an old cowboy had got a horse and ridden over there, and got the doctor and got him back here, well, you see, he'd ridden forty miles [sixty-four kilometres], and the doctor may not have been quite on time. Anyhow, it was too late!

ORCHARD: When did your father come to this country?

DEBECK: He came in '76. He came from England three years before that and stayed in Boston three years. Then he crossed the United States, I think by railroad, because there would have been railroads then, and made his way up to the coast. His first idea was to seek gold in California. Well, California was played out. He heard about the Cariboo [gold rush] and started for the Cariboo up the Fraser, you see, and heard that the Cariboo was played out.

But the last word was Cherry Creek, and he started for Cherry Creek. And he came over the Hope Mountains and he got to Cherry Creek, which might be, perhaps thirty miles [forty-eight kilometres] from here, I don't know just where. I don't know just where he would have been on the creek, and he took out a claim.

He took enough gold out of it to make my mother's wedding ring. Of course, he hadn't met her then. She didn't come to the country for another eight years, but he had this gold and it made my mother's ring and was very soft gold because it was so pure and was very heavy. She didn't wear it all the time. She didn't like to work in it. And sometimes she'd forget to put it on when she went out, and then she began to put it on only for special occasions.

ORCHARD: What was her maiden name?

DEBECK: Sophie Christine Johnson.

ORCHARD: Where did she come from?

DEBECK: She came from Peoria, Illinois.

ORCHARD: How did she come to meet your father?

DEBECK: Well, she had an uncle who was in the fur trade, and he worked from Oregon up into this valley [the Okanagan]. And he lost his wife and he went home to Peoria, and there was my mother and a cousin of hers, two young ladies about the same age. And he wanted to bring them back. Well, my mother was in a very rundown state, having lost her very beloved sister that I'm named for. And the family were rather scandalized at these young ladies starting off for this wild and woolly—

The first Hudson's Bay store in Vernon, 1897. Photo: HP009932

But they did, and I think they must have come across to Portland and up to Victoria by a construction train as far as Yale, by stage as far as Kamloops, from Kamloops to Vernon by horseback—a two-day trip stopping at Grand Prairie, which is now Westwold. The CNR [Canadian National Railway] named it Westwold.

And she rode a stock saddle, sideways. Now I've ridden a good deal, and I could ride all day long in my young days, and I thought the greatest hardship I knew of was not to be able to ride when I went to eastern school and college. But I'd hate to have ridden on a stock saddle, thirty-five miles [fifty-six kilometres], or thirty-seven or -eight miles in one day.

Cherry Creek Ranch, located between Kamloops and Savona, ca. 1908.
Photo: HP094292

It's cruel, you know! You don't fit. Of course, you had no britches. She had no divided skirt. She couldn't sit in an ordinary way in the sort of clothes they were wearing. The 1880 clothes were rather narrow with bustles. They weren't like the ones of the '70s and '60s that you might have been able to sit properly on.

They came right to Vernon, and my father hadn't seen a young lady for eight years, and she was certainly an attractive young lady—dark hair that was curly, and lovely eyes, exceedingly alert and vivacious.

Well, perhaps—vivacious—she was keen. She wasn't one of these ones that chatter. But she was highly intelligent and well educated. She had no thought of teaching school, but I think, I think it was the fall of that same year. She came in May and she said this country was a dream. It was a wet year that year, and things stayed green, and of course, there were so few houses, so few fences; it was like one park with these marvellous lakes and little streams, not spoiled in any way.

And she came, I think it was '84, eight years after Father. And I think he probably made up his mind just about like that that this young lady wasn't going to escape. And he milked his cow three times, or I don't know how many cows he had then (he probably had quite a few by then; he'd been ranching for eight years), and he milked it three times a day to take new milk to her to build her up.

And you know, up here even, when the city began to talk about having a cow in the city limits, we persisted and we had a cow as long as my mother lived, and she had new milk twice a day. We didn't have it three times a day but she—new milk was sort of the staff of life to her. She was petite, very quick and graceful in her movements, pretty hands and feet.

ORCHARD: She was living here?

DEBECK: Well, she was with the uncle down at the first Vernon Hotel, an old log building which was the trading post. The two young ladies were very shocked when they saw where their quarters were going to be. But in December, the travelling Anglican missionary or clergyman from Kamloops came down. He used to—you know, saddlebag parson—and they were married by him.

The cousin went back [to Peoria], but Mother didn't go back until '93, that was December of 1894. And she didn't go back 'til the railroad came in, the CNR. They used to call it the *Molasses Limited*, it stopped so often, and it, you know, and it only ran three times a week at first.

(6)

A Frontier Childhood

As the economy of British Columbia was tied to its natural resources, and as the gold rushes began to lose their momentum, newcomers were increasingly settling in places where they could put down roots and earn a stable income in more accessible locales. Many new townsites were established along waterways and around the railroad. The following two stories communicate two circumstances that would have been shared by thousands of children: those born in these "newly settled" lands and those who moved to British Columbia with their parents. In both anecdotes, these children, now grown, communicate a tremendous sense of motivation and an ability to navigate around a vast, and often inhospitable, terrain. They were given a remarkable amount of responsibility; however, no matter how quickly they had to grow up, their stories still manage to capture the innocence of childhood.

FACING: *Studio portrait of two young children in the 1890s.*
Photo: HP093186/Hannah Hatherly Maynard

Youngsters Haven't Got Any Fear

NELLIE BAKER

and Wild Horses in the Thompson

(RECORDED JULY 19, 1964)

NELLIE BAKER (born Ellen Elizabeth English in 1888) claims that her sister, Lillian, who was born in 1886, was the first white child born in the Chilcoten. Shortly thereafter, the family sold their ranch in the Chilcoten and moved south into the Cariboo region, near Cache Creek on the Cariboo Wagon Road, where they bought a place called Bonaparte Ranch.

Children in this area were isolated from other families, yet Baker was driven by horse and buggy to school in Cache Creek, a small town with "a few Chinese stores, and a hotel…" As she recounts earlier in the interview, "it was a stopping place when the teamsters would come up over the road." Although she was a day student, many pupils at the Cache Creek school boarded because they came from as far as Kamloops, Williams Lake, 150 Mile House, Soda Creek and Barkerville. During the winter when it was too cold to drive the eight kilometres each day to Bonaparte Ranch, Baker would sleep at the school on a straw mattress.

The school, including the dormitory, was partitioned. The fifteen to twenty boys (aged 7 to 16) sat on one side of the room while the girls sat on the other. However, the children all played ball and skated together. On Sundays, a minister came from Ashcroft to lead regular church services for the students. Baker also remembers that several children died in a scarlet fever epidemic.

As much as school may have been regimented, life on Bonaparte Ranch was quite free. Growing up on a horse ranch, Baker's passion and

FACING: *Horse and buggy days, 1895.*
Photo: H-05557

recreation centred on horses. She and her brother had free rein of the property and often got into trouble, including one episode in which they lassoed "Indian tents," wrapping the ropes around the horn of the saddle and pulling the tents down. Of course, she says, it was all in good fun!

. . .

CD3, TRACK 4

BAKER: I was born down in the Bonaparte in 1888. That would be twelve miles [nineteen kilometres] this side of Ashcroft, not far from Cache Creek.

ORCHARD: Do you remember any incidents of any kind at all when you were growing up that would be worth recalling?

BAKER: There was an awful lot of wild horses on this ranch. We must have had nearly three hundred head, wild ones, but he had his own nice horses, you know. My dad loved racehorses and good horses, and raised good ones. My brother and I, we used to go out and corral these wild horses. They, this particular band, didn't belong to us. Some of our horses probably was in among them, but we used to have an awful time to corral them they're so wild, you know—and big horses, and grown. They were around six, seven, eight, nine years old and real hard to corral.

Well, anyway, we'd chase them down off the mountain, and they'd come down. There was like two mountains, and they'd get into our pasture, like, so we'd get them down on the big flat. That'd be two and half miles [four kilometres] from where we lived, our house. It was a great big flat, and all the stock and cattle and horses used to run up there—a big lake.

So, we'd get them on the flat and then we'd steal Dad's race mares, running horses, and we'd saddle them because we couldn't—our horses wasn't fast enough to head these horses off. So we'd have these race mares all ready, you know, and then we'd saddle them up and away we'd go; and then it didn't take us very long to head these wild horses off.

Then we'd had wings built. We'd built these wings that's made out of brush and pieces of small logs, you know, rails and stuff like that, coming into a corral, like. And, they'd run against that and then they'd, we'd ease them on down into the corral. Big corrals there, and chutes in there. So we had a bunch of tin cans we'd gathered up. Oh, it took us a month to get together this big bunch of tin cans—coal-oil cans, pots, everything we could see around on the roads or wherever—we'd gather all these old tin cans. And then when we'd get these horses rounded up and in the corral, then we'd run each one in the chute and braid the tin cans up at the tail, tie it up with the tail, braid it, you know, and turned it loose—see it go buck and kick and squeal over the flat. Well, was that fun! That was just as good as a show—see those old horses. There was tin cans all over that mountain, just from us two doing crazy things like that, you know.

Oh, we even had shows out there. The boys and the girls would come from Ashcroft to see us when we'd get the animals rounded up. Of course, we lived eighteen miles [twenty-nine kilometres] from Ashcroft and just buggy and saddle horse, you know. Buggy days and saddle horse days to get there.

No, we, you know, we were just youngsters and it was just fun for us. We never got to any shows or saw anything like that. That was our fun, usually on a Sunday. Most times we'd have them corralled and let them know that we—because we couldn't always corral them. They were pretty foxy, you know. We couldn't always corral them but we usually did.

Grazing wild horses have long been a common sight in the Cariboo. Photo: FS05461-0

And Dad, one day, he was up in the racehorse pastures where he kept his racehorses, and he came home and he says, "I see these mares

A FRONTIER CHILDHOOD   147

Swimming horses across big water could be risky, Tatachuk Lake, Bella Coola Trail. Photo: HP094759/Frank Cyril Swannell

there, these two big mares." He says, "I see them all look like they've been sweating," he says, "all old dry sweat on 'em."

We never let on. We didn't tell Dad; he never knew it. From that day to this, we never did tell him. But that's what happened—just running the wild horses with his racehorses.

Horses weren't hardly worth anything—two and a half, five dollars. A real good one—maybe twenty, twenty-five. Dad used to sell a lot that went back to Alberta, Saskatchewan. The horse buyers used to come and generally come in the wintertime, in the fall. Usually in the winter they were easier to corral, but they were quite thin then, the feed not too good.

My brother and I—the Indians got a bunch of my dad's horses right across a place called Spatsum, just a little old place with a little station there. And that was just, like, three miles [five kilometres] from our place, right straight over to the Thompson River, across.

So, anyway, they sent word to Dad, and Dad sent my brother and I way down around Spences Bridge. Well, we had to go way down there, twelve miles [nineteen kilometres], and then that twelve miles back, you know, had to cross the ferry at Spences Bridge and go up. And the Indians had these horses in a corral, and they were really wild. But they helped us, and we got them out and we were going to try to drive them around, you know, down around the way we'd come from, Spences Bridge.

So anyway, my brother and I, we got our heads together. And we were just kids, barely in our teens. And, we said, we'll swim the river. We'll take them across the Thompson. So the Indians helped us but the Indians thought we'd get drowned for sure. So we got the horses in there, and they swam, and then we swam our horses across. Of course, we got wet. It was in the near wintertime, you know. It *was* winter, because there was icicles on the tails and frozen, you know.

And we got them across and brought them home, and Dad says, "My, you come awful fast. How'd you get them home?"

We said, "We come across the Thompson River by the Indian rancherie across there, the old Spatsum Rancherie."

He couldn't believe it. But, you know, I wouldn't. Today, I wouldn't do it for a million bucks. I sure wouldn't. I'd be so scared. But, you know, youngsters don't, they haven't got any fear.

. . .

IN 1915, Baker married Dr. Gerald R. "Paddy" Baker of Quesnel. Nellie soon became known as the "Florence Nightingale of the Cariboo," as she assisted in most of her husband's operations. Oftentimes, she held coal-oil lamps for doctors to operate by at night, and she was a favourite of Cariboo residents because of how far out of her way she would go to make patients feel comfortable. She often brought gifts, and she loved to offer female patients wagon rides behind her horses. She lived out her life on ranches with many animals.

anneries. Jap Boys Filling Cans.

No Children Here

WALTER WICKS

on Life as a Child at a Remote Salmon Cannery

(RECORDED JULY 20, 1961)

WALTER WICKS (b. 1894) offers insight into what a child would have experienced coming from another country, in this case Germany, to an industrial town in remote B.C. Wicks and his family immigrated to Port Edward, which was a salmon cannery town located near what is now Prince Rupert, on the Skeena River when he was six years old.

The North Pacific Cannery (est. 1889) was one of many salmon canneries located in British Columbia. In the 1890s salmon canning was one of the province's fastest-growing industries; in 1901, the peak year, over a million cases of salmon were produced. The canneries were designed as self-contained towns located in strategic locations so that the freshly caught fish could be processed as soon as possible. Thousands of people would have worked on the canning lines, and as canning was very labour intensive, these towns had clear hierarchies. Asian and Native peoples tended to make the cans and cleaned the fish. White people did the actual canning.

Although this focus on industry was good for the economy, it would not have encouraged a playful childhood. Like Nellie Baker, Wicks' account gives the impression that he was somewhat isolated as a child, that he did not have other children to play with while living at the cannery.

. . .

FACING: *Japanese boys working in a Vancouver cannery, 1913. Photo: HP084129/F. Dundas Todd*

CD3, TRACK 5

WICKS: There was a man named Fred Wicks who had been many years on the lower Skeena River, had worked around the salmon canneries. Well, he had finally decided to take a trip home and see what was left of his relatives. He went to his homeland of Germany, and there's where he met a young widow. That was my mother.

There was two of us boys. That's all the children she had. Well, they—a romance sprung up although he was a number of years older than her, and he made arrangements with her to later come out to the West Coast where they would be married.

Well, an accident happened with my brother; he got his fingers chopped off and that delayed us, but we finally prepared to leave Germany. I think it was in the month of October, 1900.

Well, we arrived at the North Pacific Cannery on the lower Skeena in a month or so later. Well, I remember it was a very beautiful moonlight night, and these impressions seem to come very vividly; the further I go back, the more clear they become. As I get older they become a little dimmer.

And when the boat pulled up alongside of the dock, the—someone was standing on the dock—an elderly man with a beard, and he had a tattered old jumper that was out at the elbows. He looked pretty rugged. I had seen the man in Germany but I couldn't recognize him now. And he shouted something across the water as the boat was warped in, and the captain shouted something back. Of course, we couldn't understand the language, neither could Mother.

Well, we later understood that he had yelled to the skipper if his family was on board, and, of course, he was assured they were all safe and sound. And Mother looked at him, and she looked at this high, foreboding mountain, back of the cannery, and she looked at the few buildings there, and she said to us boys, she says, this is our new home. Then she looked at the old man, and I could see she didn't like it. Well, anyway, we went ashore and—.

The next morning we looked around for the children to play with like boys will; we were 7 and 8 years old. But there was no children. There was no people. We had come from a large city and we asked, "Where are the children?" Well there are no children here. The cannery is closed for

Fresh Skeena River salmon was packed into cans at the Inverness Cannery and shipped worldwide, ca. 1900s. Photo: I-6111

the season until next spring and there are only a handful of Japanese woodcutters here. They cut cordwood for the canneries for the following spring because everything then was done by hand. Cans were made by hand, and cordwood was used and some coal shipped in.

And then preparations were made for them to go and get a preacher. Well that was up the river sixteen miles [twenty-five kilometres] to Port Essington. That was the closest. So we got into a boat, an open fishboat. There was no powerboats those days. Gasoline boat engines were never heard of. And we piled into a double-ender fishing boat and set sail with the tide and went up the river for sixteen miles, I believe it was—about there—to Port Essington, where arrangements were made and they were married there by a, the Reverend Appleyard was his name.

Well, we stayed with the Adams family that night. His name was Jimmy Adams. He was an old-timer on the river. And during the evening celebration, why, many of the old-timers were there, including Bob Cunningham, the founder of the town, the old trader. And someone had taken a can and big coal-oil can, five gallons, filled it with rocks and hauled it up and down the roof on the end of a line. This was part of the celebration, and a lot of noise was made—shotguns were blasted off—and in the next morning we saw Jimmy patching up the shingles on the roof. So we asked our new stepdad what he had said, so he translated to us that Jimmy had muttered something about the white man would do well to take lessons in good behaviour from the Indians. He didn't like the way his roof had been torn up with these cans.

Well, then we went down the river. The river is divided into three arms. We lived on the north arm called, known as the Inverness Slough. The old name has still stuck in spite of the fact that they later on changed it to North Skeena Passage. The Inverness Slough still sticks [the slough is now known as Inverness Passage]. We got down there at the head of the slough; we got stuck on the sandbar, and there we stuck for four hours. Often, years later, Mother would be talking to other of her women friends and they would speak about their honeymoon, and she said, "Yes, I spent my honeymoon in a stinking fish bar, fishboat, on the sandbar, for four hours in the drizzling rain."

And, however, we had to stay there that winter, and everything, of course, was new and venturesome to us boys. The deer on the beach, and the wild ducks and geese flying by, but we were lonesome for companionship. And Mother had no woman to talk to, and there we were 'til early spring—before the cannery crew came up—without any outside contact you might say. With only an occasional coastal vessel coming in to take some salmon off from the cannery and take it down the coast. Only the Japanese woodcutters.

The cannery did spring up in the spring of the year, early May or April. The crews would come up, and the Chinese crews would come and make cans by hand. The cordwood had been burnt into charcoal during the winter months, besides what was cut for the boilers. And coppers were used, hand coppers heated in these little charcoal stoves to solder up the cans when they made them and when they—and how they sealed them up with the salmon and during the season.

We took everything in, and of course, everything was so new and exciting to us. When the first salmon came and was spilled on the floor, Stepdad would take us two kids by the hand, you know, and he would walk us right through the cannery and show us every phase of the canning business. And right from the time the fish were first washed, to the time the label was put on and boxed up.

And, of course, the question of schooling had come up quite often during the winter. I may be a little ahead of myself, but they were packing up to send us to the Metlakatla missionary home, boarding home, which was the closest place Essington had—. Port Essington, let me say, had a school, but often it wasn't easy to make contact there, when the river got full of ice and would plug the river up for twenty, thirty, forty miles [thirty, fifty, sixty kilometres]. So they sent us further north, up the coast, to the old village of Metlakatla. That was Metlakatla, British Columbia. Metlakatla, Alaska, was formed, had been formed also. But, finally a man came along up in the boat and he said, "There'd be no use you sending your two boys to Metlakatla school." He said, "The village just burnt down." Well that put us back seven months.

When a new home was built, and we were placed in it that following year, so we had a chance to see the cannery in operation before we got to school. By that time I was now 8 years old.

We attended the school and boarded in the missionary home there for, I think it was three years or a little better. Then a school was formed for the first time at the Inverness Cannery, a mile and a half downriver below us. At that time, I think it needed six children to start a school. Now we had about eight or ten, and we attended school there. And I was attending school there for about a year, year and a half.

Anyway, I got to as far as what you would now call the fifth grade. First and second primer; first, second and third reader is as far as I got. That's all the education I've had to this day. I've never been to a night school or anything since, because they put me in a fishing boat at the age of 13. And those boats, those days were all sails and oars. There was no powerboats of any kind. We had no cabins. The only protection we had in real bad weather was a little pup tent, that is, would be the equivalent to the pup tent of today.

Otherwise, it was just hard, backbreaking work, and as a boy of 13, I became a man many years before my age. And there were many instances that I could relate of our adventures on the water in the fishing business, and I don't right know where you would want me to continue.

(7)

Legendary Figures and Historical Characters

BRITISH COLUMBIA'S history is rich with colourful characters, from such well-known political figures as Governor James Douglas and Judge Matthew Begbie, to folk heroes–criminals such as Bill Miner. Many of the province's legendary names have long been forgotten or, at least, underplayed. The firsthand stories in the Orchard Collection remind us of many of these earlier personalities and breathe new life into the people and events that shaped the province.

FACING: *"Gentlemanly" George Edwards, alias Bill Miner, upon his capture at Kamloops, 1906.* Photo: HP003761

More Trader Than Missionary

AGNES HARRIS

on Robert Cunningham and the Founding of Port Essington

(RECORDED FEBRUARY 8, 1962)

ROBERT CUNNINGHAM (1837–1905) founded the town of Port Essington on the south bank of the Skeena River between Terrace and Prince Rupert in northwestern B.C. Born in Dungannon, Ireland, Cunningham came to Canada in 1862 at age 25 with the Anglican Church Missionary Society to work with William Duncan at Metlakatla. Two years later, in 1864, Cunningham left the mission to work for the Hudson's Bay Company (HBC) at Fort Simpson, where he became chief trader before leaving the company in 1870.

His first wife was a Tsimshian woman named Elizabeth Ryan who drowned in 1888 when the canoe she and Reverend Sheldon were using to try to help a sick Native person split in two. He and Ryan had five children together; however, only two of them survived childhood. In 1893, Cunningham married again, and he and Flora Bicknell had three more children.

The following story is told by Agnes Harris (b. 1885), who came to Canada from England in 1905 with her husband, Arthur George Harris, whom she'd met while he was visiting his family—as he did every five years—in the Old Country. Arthur Harris had met Robert Cunningham during his first trip to Canada in 1889, and their friendship was one of the reasons that the Harrises settled in Port Essington, also known as Cunningham's Town. As the largest centre in the area, Port Essington

FACING: *Port Essington, 1890s.*
Photo: HP010714/Maynard

became an important fishing and cannery town with a very strong Japanese and Aboriginal presence.

After his death, Cunningham was buried at Metlakatla.

. . .

CD3, TRACK 6

HARRIS: Robert Cunningham came out from Ireland, sent out for the Church Missionary Society as a lay missionary. He came out from Ireland in the early '60s. Well, he didn't stay very long with them. He joined the Hudson's Bay Company at Port Simpson. He was Factor there for some time, and he was a born trader more than a missionary and he thought he would like to make, go into business for himself.

And he looked 'round and found this spot on the Skeena. It was called Spaksuut by the Indians. That estuary was called Port Essington, named by Captain Vancouver for one of, Admiral Essington, of the Royal Navy. And he took that name and put to the place that he founded. He found this was a good spot. And he induced an Indian family to come there, and he said, now he was going to have supplies come up. And, of course, they had to come up on the *Otter*, the old Hudson's Bay ship, the only ship going up there at that time.

So he said, "Now, make the captain think there's quite a place here."

So they lit bonfires and they put a lot of red bits of red flannel, like flags, up in the trees. And when Mr. Cunningham's first supplies came up, well, it looked as though there was someplace already established, you see. And, so that's how he started.

Robert Cunningham's chickamin.
Photo: HP027754

He built a store. That was in 1872. And he built a store and hotel, salmon cannery, sawmill. He had tugboats, and eventually riverboats to go up to Hazelton. Before that, he would help man the canoes to go up to Hazelton to get the furs and so on.

And they had quite a big sawmill. In fact, when Prince Rupert was started, they supplied the lumber for the first wharf, and their piledriver drove the first piles in for the original wharf.

Oh, it was quite a place. The miners would come in, down in the wintertime, and they would stay at Port Essington and they would bring their gold dust, you see.

Well, Robert Cunningham, of course—it was a long way from where there was any bank, and proper coinage wasn't used there for a long time. And so he did the same as the Hudson Bay had done. He had got copper and had a die and made the copper coinage—a dollar, fifty cents and quarters—with his own initial on, you see. And that was good for trade in his store. And he would give that to the Indians for their furs and so on, to be traded back to him for goods. And it all worked out profitably for him and also quite all right for the Indians. They used that for many years.

The first, first bank there, I think, was in 1906. Of course, then, they were thinking of bringing the new railway in, but one incident connected with that. When the CPR was being surveyed, they weren't sure whether the Fraser or the Skeena would be the river that would come to the coast. So a survey party went all down the Skeena River to the coast, and they employed Indians as guides and they paid them with paper money, Canadian dollars. The Indians looked at this—it wasn't worth much. It would tear. It was no good. They took it to Mr. Cunningham and wanted his *chickamin* [the Chinook word for metal money], as they called it. Of course, he was only too glad to change over. It went back to him in trade too, so everyone was satisfied with that!

Robert Cunningham at Port Essington.
Photo: HP052047

He Was a Robin Hood

MARTIN STARRET

on the Capture of Bill Miner, the Legendary Train Robber

(RECORDED MARCH 24, 1963)

THE FOLLOWING two anecdotes are provided by a resident of Hope named Martin Stevens Starret (1888–1973). He is an amazing resource for anecdotes about the Hope area, all the way up to the Babine. In fact, of Orchard's 998 interviews, the longest of all was with Starret. Over the course of several recording sessions, the interviews with Starret totalled 1,230 minutes (twenty and a half hours) in a seven-year period! Not only was Starret a great source of history, as his experiences took him all over the province, but he was a gifted storyteller with marvellous recall. His stories reveal a real feel for people's characters and show Starret to be a keen observer. Best of all, he was blessed with exactly the type of speaking voice—simultaneously gravelly and playful—that one would expect in a font of pioneer lore.

His work as a fur trader, among many other jobs, brought him into contact with many people all over British Columbia. At the age of 21, he and his mother operated a trading post at the "Indian village" at the bottom of Babine Lake. After obtaining a pre-emption near Stuart Lake, he became an assistant ranger for the B.C. Forest Service in the 1930s. In fact, Starret Lake in the Babine area is named for him. The Babine Nation gave Martin Starret the name Chinnikh, which means "marten," the small animal—an appropriate name for a fur trader. Starret spoke Babine, Chinook as well as a few other bits of languages.

FACING: *The posse that caught Bill Miner, May 1906.*
Photo: HP032163

The first of Starret's anecdotes is about the famous train robber Bill Miner who was active in the first decade of the 1900s. Miner has been the subject of numerous books and a full-length motion picture, *The Grey Fox*. Known as "The Gentlemen Bandit," Miner was perceived as a kind of Robin Hood who would give money to children or those in need, and he is reputed to have originated the phrase "Hands up!" so that he did not have to shoot a gun or kill anyone.

Miner was born in either 1842 or 1847 in Bowling Green, Kentucky, and served time at San Quentin State Prison near San Francisco in the late 1800s before moving to Princeton, British Columbia, in November 1903. He presented himself as George W. Edwards, a Texan gentleman in search of peace and compatible climate. After settling in on his friend Jack Budd's ranch, Edwards met William "Shorty" Dunn. The two men robbed a train at Mission Junction in September 1904. No one in Princeton would have suspected the gentlemanly and popular Edwards, who often wowed people with his fiddling skills. In November 1905, around the same time he built a skating rink for some local children, another Great Northern train was held up near Seattle, Washington.

Sometime in 1906, Louis Colquhoun arrived at the Budd ranch. On May 8, 1906, Edwards, Dunn and Colquhoun targeted a gold-bearing train near Ducks (today called Monte Creek), just east of Kamloops. In the end, the car did not contain any gold, and the three men only made off with a package of liver pills and fifteen dollars in cash. Starret describes how these men, posing as prospectors, were eventually caught.

. . .

CD3, TRACK 7

STARRET: "By the way, one of those pack horses," one of the packers told me, "You see that bull-faced rune horse over there? His name is Bill Miner. That's the horse that had the split hoof that they tracked from where they held up the train at Ducks. Bill Miner did out in toward the Okanagan there. He had no shoes on the split hoof. That's the horse right there that the police tracker followed 'til they found the camp where Bill Miner was." Rune horse I believe, just the same as any other cayuse.

ORCHARD: What was the story about that? Tell us it from the beginning about the horse or about Bill Miner.

STARRET: Well, Bill Miner was the famous train robber, and the first we know of him, he came up this road from Chilliwack, I guess, from Westminster somewhere, leading a burro, supposed to have been. Maybe it was a cross between a donkey and a cayuse. And over the trail to Princeton. And he was a prospector. He didn't tell anybody who he was, of course. And he was a good man. He was good to everybody. He was a Robin Hood. Anybody was poor, why he'd help 'em. He'd—

And, I remember I was 14 at the time and I'd killed a deer down here about a mile, and I was bringing him out of the bush one morning to the old Yale Road to take down home to Silver Creek. I was dragging it out. There was a little snow on the road, and four saddle horses came down the hill there, what's now Watkins Hollow. One of them was Bill Miner. Then there was Shorty Dunn and Colquhoun, and, I think, Jack Budd or some more ranchers from Princeton that weren't mixed in it at all—they just happened to be going down there, and Miner was with them.

Well, Miner and this Dunn or Colquhoun or some of them would pull this robbery at Mission that same winter, just a few weeks after. And they got away in a motorboat. I don't know where they went, or they think they did.

The reward notice for the arrest and conviction of the four men who robbed the CPR train between Ducks and Kamloops on May 6, 1906. Photo: HP066920

The town of Princeton in Bill Miner's day, ca. 1900s. Photo: I-55696

Well then, apparently he drifted back again to Princeton the next spring and, well, he belonged there. Naturally the prospector would go back, and nothing was thought about it. And it seems to me the next was that, was that robbery of Ducks out from Kamloops.

I was in Princeton at the time, and he was from Princeton. He was known as George Edwards. I didn't know him personally. I was a kid and he was a grown-up. But then I knew of him, and some of the boys right there in Princeton, Vic Rider, George Warler, some of them, they went off to hunt these train robbers. They didn't know who it was, of course. But they didn't find him, but the police had got an Indian tracker had followed this split hoof way out to the mountains and then, then there wouldn't have, there wouldn't have been anything but this Dunn was with him, this Shorty Dunn. When he see the police he got panicky and ran for the guns. Darn fool!

When they see this old prospector, Bill Miner. He says, "Hello boys! Good morning! Come and have a cup of coffee." It would have been all right. I don't think they'd've ever tumbled.

But this other fella got panicky, you see. And that was it. The jig was up!

Then they put him in Westminster or Keller or somewhere, and he said he'd be out pretty soon. He was out again. Yeah.

ORCHARD: How did they track, where were they tracking this split hoof from?

STARRET: Kamloops or Ducks. Somewhere, someplace, station out of Kamloops. I don't know whether it's this side of Kamloops. It must be the other side. Somewhere around the side of Monte Creek or somewhere over there.

ORCHARD: From where the second robbery was made they—

STARRET: Yes. Well, there was, I think there was another robbery in between. I forget where that was.

ORCHARD: Well, I think there was one down in the States somewhere—

STARRET: Yeah, before he came, and then there was either two or three here. And he told them they wouldn't stay in there long. And they didn't either; he just walked out. How, I don't know. That's none of my business. I guess they let him out, they saw he was such a good fella. I don't know. He got out anyway. He'd pretend to be very religious, always reading his bible.

And one time he was coming over in the fall. Yeah, that was the same fall. 1903. Fall of 1903. And he got in and left the lake house in the morning quite early. It was still dark when he got the rig on the horses and got going, and he got down here just as kids were going to school. And he went into Wartles store and he saw the kids going, "Got any candy in the pail over there?"

"Yeah I got the pail half full."

"Well, give me that!"

And he runs out. "Here, have some candy, children! Make ya feel better going to school this morning. Take lots. Put some in your pocket." He brought the pail in, paid the bill and I guess the pail was empty. I forget how that went, but that was him.

. . .

BILL MINER escaped from the New Westminster jail in 1907. He fled to the United States where he worked in mines and once again posed as a southern gentleman in search of health. In 1911 Miner, posing as George Anderson this time, committed the first-ever train robbery in the state of Georgia with two accomplices. He was arrested two days later and scheduled for deportation back to New Westminster, where he claims to have been treated kindly. In the end, the Georgia officials decided to hold him to serve on a chain gang. A few months after, Miner and a fellow prisoner escaped once again but were soon caught. His final escape came in 1912, when, during a thunderstorm, Miner cut his shackles, sawed his prison bars and fled. Once again he was caught. Miner died in a prison hospital on September 2, 1913. He was in his late sixties, or early seventies. Miner's friends paid for his funeral. The dates on his tombstone, which was bought for him in 1964, are incorrect.

There's Old Cataline

MARTIN STARRET

on B.C.'s Most Famous Mule Packer

(RECORDED MARCH 24, 1963)

JEAN CAUX, better known as Cataline, worked as a packer in British Columbia from 1858 until his retirement in 1912, a span of fifty-four years. He originally came from southern California, where, hearing that gold had been discovered on the Fraser River, he organized a pack train and drove north to the Fraser, at which point he joined forces with a Mexican packer named Jesus Cristo Marino. Together they reached the Fraser while the mining was still confined to the lower river.

Cataline's pack trains supplied a large portion of the province: no settlement was too remote and no mineral discovery too inaccessible for him, and he never failed to deliver his cargo. Even though Cataline was illiterate, he was keenly aware of what goods each of his sixty mules was carrying, where they were going and how much to charge for each load.

Cataline was easily recognizable in his broad-brimmed sombrero, fur, heavy woolen trousers and dainty riding boots, and he always had a silk handkerchief tied around his neck. His reputation was legendary; however, there were three things of which he himself was very proud: his Spanish origin, his Canadian citizenship and the fact that he had, for years, been a friend of Judge Matthew Baillie Begbie. When he died in 1922, he was close to 100 years old. His body is buried in an unmarked grave in the Native village overlooking Hazelton.

. . .

ABOVE: *The famous packer Jean Caux, Cataline, with a crew in 1897 heading to Babine Lake.* Photo: HP008760

ORCHARD: What do you remember of Cataline?

STARRET: Oh, I was too young to drink with Cataline. I'm not a drinking man anyway, but I've seen other fellows. I've seen other fellows there.

And they'd say, "Hey, Cataline! Come on. Have a drink."

"For you for me?"

"Yep. You for me. Sure. You and me."

"All right."

And they said that he'd drink his drink and always leave a little in the bottom, and he'd pour that in his left hand and then wipe it on his head. That was just a curiosity, or a fad of his that I don't suppose it did his hair any good, but then he imagined that was a good way.

And Cataline wasn't his name. His name was Jean Caux but he used the word "cataline." For instance, at the bunch string of horses going along or mules on the trail, and they'd come to a hill and there'd about ten of them up on this hill, and they'd stop and get their wind when they get out of wind there. They'd all be standing there. Well then that's holding the whole darn train up.

Cataline'd be sitting back there, and when they think it about time for these mules to start again he'd say, "Hey there! Cataline!"

And then them old mules would flip their ears back and forward and start then, when he'd holler, "Cataline!"

So that's the name he went by.

ORCHARD: Why would he say "cataline"? You don't know, have no idea?

STARRET: Well he was supposed to have been, maybe he was able to say that. His language was, as Sperry Cline [a constable, and another person that Imbert Orchard interviewed] said, was a jargon: some Chinook and some English and some Spanish, I suppose.

I think it was 1910 or '11—it doesn't matter which much—but I was heading down to the Hudson Bay store or warehouse, probably to see about some freight for C.V. Smith, my uncle, the fur trader in Hazelton, and I happened to be walking along and I fell in with Cataline. His train was gathered on the street; they took the entire street there, the outfit was right there loading up. Oh I suppose they had sixty head of mules and horses, and probably six, seven packers there. They were just getting the stuff out there. The mules were there, and there was a fellow tinkering with a horse there—with his feet, shoeing the horse. One of these tall Mongolian guys.

And he says, "Hey Tong! You see that, you see that jenny over there, black one. The little one, this side. You take 'em all shoe off that mule. Take 'em all off!"

"You mean you want new shoes?"

"No! Leave 'em off! Two, four case of eggs go Babine, and put 'em one packing eggs, that mule."

And then he turns to me and he says, "No shoe, he go out there and maybe ten miles [sixteen kilometres], fifteen miles [twenty-four kilometres], his feet get sore. He walk easy just like a cat and not break one egg!" Yeah, he shook his—, "Not break one egg!" he said.

He shook a finger at me. He made signs with his two hands, "He walk just like ze cat," he says. "Not break one egg going down the hill the other side."

He wouldn't go down hard on not—when he get going down the other slope, you know, toward the lake.

He couldn't. I don't suppose he could read or write. He kept everything in his head, his accounts straight as a die. And he came into that country, you know, and brought all that rigging on those animals with him.

The last time I saw him was in the office of Doctor Wrinch's office. You know, the Wrinch Memorial Hospital. Doctor Wrinch was a man of about fifty and he'd just been examining me. I had a goiter on my neck, and he kind of pushed me out. And here was Cataline.

"Hey, Cataline! You back again?"

"Yeah, yeah. I sick today."

"Well, you been drinking?"

"Oh, just port wine."

"You cut that out. I told you before. Don't you drink port wine or anything else. You can't take it anymore."

"Yeah."

"Well, I can't do anything for you."

"Well, I sick stomach."

Cataline's pack train on the main street in Barkerville, 1868.
Photo: HP056819/Frederick Dally

"Well, I'll give you something to fix that sick stomach. You keep away from that drinking. I told you before."

The summer of 1917, in August, automobiles were running then. From south Hazelton—there was a bridge right there over to Hazelton in those days—and I was in an auto. And I remember from the direction of Mission Point, toward Hazelton, I think it was on the Hazelton side of the Bulkley River. He was walking toward town very slowly, and I said to somebody in that car (it was an old Model T Ford, you know). I said, "By gosh! There's old Cataline. He must be pretty nearly a hundred years old."

That was August 1917. He only lasted a little while after that. You could see he was old.

The Hanging Judge

TOM CAROLAN

on Matthew Begbie's Frontier Justice

(RECORDED IN 1964)

THOMAS JESS CAROLAN (1905–1982) was an expert on settlement life in the Cariboo between 1850 and 1930. Born in Alberta, he was riding horses by the age of 5 and wandered all over that province with his family as part of a wagon train of settlers moving with their cattle and horses. Carolan lived in many places, including Glecian, but grew up in Consort, Alberta, until he "wandered into the Cariboo" when he was 16 years old to work as a cowboy. He settled in Williams Lake and reputedly knew everyone in the city and the surrounding area, which is how he became an expert about the region. He met Cataline in 1921. A year later, Carolan married Isabella Mary Pinchbeck (1902–1969), granddaughter of William Pinchbeck (1831–1893) who was one of the original settlers of the Cariboo region in 1860.

Pinchbeck was a key figure around Williams Lake, as he was a police officer and gold commissioner, and owned many properties including a flour mill, distillery, roadhouse and horse-racing track. Like most police officers of his time, he acted as judge, jailer, lawyer and justice of the peace. Pinchbeck's company eventually owned almost all of the Williams Lake Valley. Carolan donated many of William Pinchbeck's ledgers and journals to the Williams Lake archives in the 1930s.

The central character in this story, however, is Sir Matthew Baillie Begbie (1819–1894). Born and raised in Britain, he reached Fort Victoria in 1858 and was sworn into office as the first official judge in British

FACING: *William Pinchbeck, gold commissioner and policeman, ca. 1880. Photo: HP006865/Spencer and Hastings*

Columbia in Fort Langley in 1885, on the day that British Columbia was proclaimed a colony. He was also British Columbia's first citizen, sworn in by Governor James Douglas before he affirmed Douglas himself. As a judge—and later as Chief Justice of the Supreme Court until his death—Begbie was charged with establishing law and order in the new colony. To do this, he travelled all over the colony by horseback or on foot, wearing his judicial robes and wigs and holding court in many makeshift courtrooms.

In the popular imagination, Begbie is known as "The Hanging Judge" because of his reputation for meting out harsh penalties. The death penalty was mandatory in murder cases in the time that Begbie was presiding, and he did rule on fifty-two cases in which men were hung. However, he argued for clemency in several cases where murder was accused. Also somewhat contrary to his reputation for ruthlessness, he espoused the rights of Chinese and Native people. Finally, Begbie, with Douglas, played a key role in making sure that the colony remained British, which was quite a task considering the huge influx of Americans coming into the area.

Carolan served with the Canadian Air Force during the Second World War. He is buried on Galiano Island.

. . .

CD3, TRACK 9

CAROLAN: There were seventeen people hung at Williams Lake. I guess you knew that, didn't you? Begbie hung seventeen at Williams Lake. And the gallows were still there just a few years ago.

Up about three miles [five kilometres] there's a place that, in latter years, I always knew as the Comer Ranch. Well, that was the original Pinchbeck Ranch, and I think there's part of that house standing. Well, that's where the executions went on and that's where Judge Begbie held court.

There was a fellow one time at the 150 Mile House, the story goes—that was in the days of Judge Begbie—and he had caught—he had shot a man right out in the middle of the street, the road, in front of the, it was as they called it in them days, the gin mill. And somebody told him he couldn't do that.

And he said, "Well, I can do as I like."

So, he was taken to the—He started out on the right-hand side of the lake to the William's Lake place, and they sent an Indian on the south side of the lake. And he told Old Man Pinchbeck, who was the gold commissioner and the policeman and everything that went.

And this fellow came in and asked for a drink, and they gave him a drink.

And then he said, "Another one."

And they said, "How about paying for the first one?"

He said, "I don't pay for anything. I just killed a man because he talked back to me."

Old Man Pinchbeck was known to never carry a gun. He carried a lead scaleweight in his hip pocket with a piece of rawhide thong on it. So he just—how he did it I don't know—but apparently he tied this fellow up and put him in the back room. And that day Judge Begbie was coming back from his summer tour to Barkerville.

So when he came in—now I got this from Pinchbeck's son, who was a boy, well, a young man.

And he said, when he came in, Old Pinchbeck said, "Well, Judge, I got a murderer here for you."

So Judge Begbie says, "Well, we'll try him this afternoon."

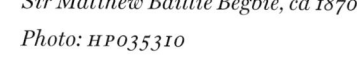

Sir Matthew Baillie Begbie, ca 1870.
Photo: HP035310

So he went outside and said, "I want twelve men." He said, "I want a jury."

So he called the twelve and got twelve men in, and they tried this fellow and they had to continue until after dinner. They still had to have some more witnesses so they continued on after dinner, and about nine o'clock that night they decided that it was over. The jury decided he was guilty.

Judge Begbie says, "Take him out and hang him at daylight tomorrow morning."

And he was hung. And that's why we never had an American West in British Columbia. Absolutely—there's no argument about that.

LEGENDARY FIGURES & HISTORICAL CHARACTERS

The Queen of Kitselas

WIGGS O'NEILL

on a Bizarre Bootlegging Trial

(RECORDED JULY 9, 1961)

WILLIAM JOHN "Wiggs" O'Neill (1882–1963) was a great storyteller from the Skeena River area, and Imbert Orchard interviewed him twice in the summer of 1961, for a total of six hours. Born in Barkerville, O'Neill grew up in Port Simpson (now Lax Kw'alaams) after his family moved there in 1892. He worked many jobs, including as a baker, farmer, purser on the steamship *Inlander*, telegraph line worker, land clearer for the townsite of Smithers and builder of the first electric light plant in Smithers in 1913. In his later years, he became the foremost historian on steamships of the Skeena River and wrote two books on the subject: *Steamboat Days on the Skeena River* and *Whitewater Men of the Skeena*. O'Neill also co-authored (with Sergeant Sperry Cline), a book entitled *Along The Totem Trail: Port Essington to Hazelton*. In 1953, he ran for the Progressive Conservative Party in the 24th British Columbia election. Finally, Wiggs Creek, located outside of Smithers, is named in his honour.

In this story, O'Neill tells the story of a Native woman known only as The Queen of Kitselas. The town of Kitselas, which means "people of the village at the canyon," is located upriver from the city of Terrace, at the upper end of the Kitselas Canyon on the Skeena River. The Kitselas people for whom the town is named are one of fourteen tribes of the Tsimshian Nation that has occupied the valley for ten thousand years. Although it was suggested, after the Grand Trunk Pacific Railway came

FACING: *Kitselas, located on the Skeena River, means "people of the village at the canyon" in Tsimshian. Photo:* HP076170 through, that the town be renamed Vanarsdol for C.C. Van Arsdoll, an engineer, the original name has stuck.

O'Neill mentions Chinook jargon several times during his anecdote. This trade language originated in the Pacific Northwest and is related to, but not the same as, the language used by the Chinook Nation that lived along the Columbia River in present-day Washington and Oregon. Consisting of a simple vocabulary of common words, the jargon, which consisted of Chinook, Salishan and Nootka languages among others (and eventually took on bits of English and French as well), allowed people from many diverse language families to communicate. It is estimated that over 100,000 people used this jargon in the pre-war era. Today, several words from this jargon are common in the English language, including aha, potlatch and skookum, which means "good" or "strong." A skookum house, therefore, is a strong house, or jail.

. . .

CD3, TRACK 10

O'NEILL: Before the railway came to Kitselas, it was a very small place. Oh, there couldn't have been maybe more than a dozen old prospector shacks, and Hudson Bay had a warehouse there because they often had to discharge summer freight there. And they had the only boats on the river.

There was just a few living around there that prospected, and there's only one woman in town—an old Indian woman who they called Kitselas Liz. And she was quite an old character. She used to do the washing around town for these prospectors, and so on, but outside of that it was a very quiet place.

And in 1910, when they started to build the Grand Pacific Railway, things changed. Kitselas became a very important centre. Stores sprung up, a hotel and a magistrate there, and it was important as a little town. And things were fairly quiet yet. Things were springing up. And one day there was an Indian girl arrived from town—quite a comely lass and very quiet. Nobody ever heard her speak.

So one day it came to the magistrate's ears that she was doing a little bit of bootlegging, and he couldn't believe it because she was such a well-behaved person and caused no trouble or anything. So he thought it was probably just idle talk. And they hadn't appointed a policeman yet in Kitselas, but they had appointed one at Kitsumkalum, down the river about ten miles [sixteen kilometres]. His name was Tom Parsons. Kitselas hadn't become important enough to have a policeman yet.

Anyway, he finally—the magistrate had a complaint registered by the contractor across the river on the second tunnel, the "Big Rock" tunnel. And he said that the Queen of Kitselas had got over there. That was the name that people had begun to call her, the Queen of Kitselas. So got over there and had a stock of liquor with her, and put his whole camp on a spree—and work all stopped which was quite important. So he had to do something about it, so he sent down to Kitsumkalum to Tom Parsons and asked him to come up. So he came up, and he told him the story.

So the water was very high in the river, so Tom hired a man with—who had a canoe, a good canoe man. And they couldn't cross the river right at the canyon because it was too turbulent, so they had to haul the canoe up the river on the road by horse and team, and put it in the water above the canyon—well up so it wouldn't be drawn into the canyon—and get across.

B.C. Provincial Police Commissioner Tom W.S. Parsons, 1930s. Photo: I-68628

LEGENDARY FIGURES & HISTORICAL CHARACTERS

So they finally walked down the grade and arrested the Queen in her lair, number two tunnel. Brought her across to Kitselas and threw her into the skookum house. They built a little skookum house there—about ten by ten out of two by fours—to be in readiness when they did get a policeman. And so they threw her in the skookum house. She was the first customer they had there.

So it was quite an important case. And the magistrate felt that he should be very careful with it, and so he sent down to Kitsumkalum (where Terrace is today) and asked the Reverend Marsh if he'd come up and give him a hand—because Reverend Marsh was a JP [Justice of the Peace], and with the two of them on the case, they might come to a better decision.

So Mr. Marsh came up, and finally the court was opened in the schoolhouse, the Queen was put on the stand. And Tom Parsons' charges her with being, supplying liquor against the law—and asked her if she was guilty or not guilty. And she just looked at him with a stone face and never a word came out of her mouth. And he asked her several times and she didn't answer.

So Mr. Clifford, the magistrate, he had been an old Hudson Bay man all his life and he was quite proficient in talking Chinook, so he tried her out in Chinook. Same thing. Just a stone stare. No answer.

So the Reverend Marsh, he had spent a good many years in the Cree country, in Blackfoot country in the Northwest Territories and in northern Alberta, so he was quite proficient in Cree. So he tried Cree on her. Same thing. No response.

So the law men were in a kind of a quandary. They didn't know what to do. They finally, come to conclusion that she must be unfortunate and be deaf and dumb. And so, well they had to do something about it, so finally—they thought they'd have to set an example anyways.

So the magistrate said, "Well, young lady. We have to find you guilty. You can't speak in your defence, so we fine you fifty dollars in costs and bind you over to keep the peace."

So the Queen reached under her shawl and she pulled out a great big, a black handkerchief, all tied up in knots. And she started in, untying the knots and finally she came out with quite a bank roll. And she peeled off five ten-dollar bills and shoved them across the desk to the magistrate.

And she said, "Thank you, Your Honour." And she walked out the front door.

And the policeman and the magistrate and the JP all looked at each other. Finally, the magistrate found his voice and he said, "Well, I'll be damned."

The preacher he said, "Well, you can let that go for me, too."

Tom Parsons said, "Well, count me in, too."

So they found out later on that the Queen of Kitselas had had a very good education, been educated in one of the mission schools down the coast someplace and was quite capable of talking. But, no doubt, she was foxy.

BONUS TRACK

Busting Comrades Out of the Clink

ARTHUR SHELFORD
Recounts a Jailbreak

(RECORDED NOVEMBER 9, 1961)

THE INTERVIEW with Arthur Shelford is exceptional because he simply spoke and told his story. There are tangents of well over thirty minutes in which Orchard does not even speak; Shelford just flows. This story is part of the same interview in which Shelford discusses Jack Norman, the Norwegian foreman from his time on the extra gang outside Field, B.C. (see Chapter 2). In this tangent, Shelford highlights the bonds of friendship not only between fellow workers but the caring shown by their bosses out in the field. What's more, he reveals that while the police were trying to do their job, workers were often finding tricky ways to get away with something.

In this anecdote, Shelford mentions that the Royal Canadian Mounted Police, or RCMP, enforced the law near Field in 1908. However, he really means the Royal Northwest Mounted Police (RNWMP), which was founded in 1873. This force and the Dominion Police (founded in 1868) merged in 1920 to form today's RCMP. The "hoosegow" is a slang term of Spanish origin for a jail; it is similar in meaning to the clink, the slammer, the pokey or the big house.

. . .

SHELFORD: There was one incident I should like to remark about after I left the extra gang.

CD3, TRACK 11

FACING: *A group of Mounties.*
Photo: *HP082942*

I said Norman was a good man, good foreman; he was a good man, too. A few days after I left, the Scotchmen on the gang, they got drunk. They got picked up by the North West Mounted Police, and they got put in the hoosegow! But one of them didn't get put in. He wasn't drunk, I suppose: Sandy McIver. He showed up to have a look at his comrades in the clink, and in those days the prisoners could get out into cages outside. And Sandy found some keys hanging up on the wall outside, so what did he do but let the prisoners loose. Unfortunately, he couldn't find the key to one of the cells, and he couldn't let McKinley loose.

Well, McKinley was still in his cups a little, and when the RCMP got after him and pressured him to say who let the prisoners out, he said, "Sandy McIver." 'Course, the police went down to the gang.

But, in the meantime, Norman had been busy.

He said, "How'd you fellows get out?" when they all trooped down there.

"Oh, Sandy come and let us out."

"Good God!" said Norman. "Sandy, you did that? Well, those bulls will be down here, and they'll get you right away. Now here, come to the office," took him to the office. Aye!

He signed Sandy McIver off and he changed his name to Jock Scott. Jock Scott was still on the gang, but Sandy McIver had gone along the track. In due course, the police did come down. They wanted Sandy McIver.

"I paid him off, and he's gone along the track."

"All right. Line your men up."

Norman lined the men up. The police went to Sandy McIver and they said, "What's your name?"

"Jock Scott."

That was that. They got away with it. But Norman said to Sandy, he said, "Look here, Sandy. You're my best man and I hate to lose you, but," he said, "it's no good you stopping here. Somewhere they'll get you."

So Sandy did have to go down the track, but he didn't go with the police. I've often wondered whether in this case, whether the North West Mounted Police *did* get their man. But that is the last I ever heard of it.

EPILOGUE

Bringing the Orchard Collection Full Circle

IAN STEPHEN

(RECORDED NOVEMBER 23, 2009)

IAN WILLIAM McLean Stephen (b. January 19, 1925) worked with Imbert Orchard in the field as both the recording technician and on-the-fly editor for Orchard's radio programs. However, although details of Orchard's biography are easy to find, archival records, birth records, obituaries and cemetery records revealed nothing—not even a birth date—for Stephen. As it turns out, without meaning to, Orchard had thrown me off the track. He was a member of Subud, a spiritual movement, which subsequently led him to change his name from Robert to Imbert. As a show of playful affection, and with Stephen's nodding approval, Orchard wrote "Ean" rather than Ian on all the tapes, which is why I was never able to find him.

Fortunately, just as I was literally three days from submitting the final proofs of this book, Colin Preston at CBC Archives called to say that he'd discovered Ian Stephen alive and well and living in Campbell River, B.C.—about three hours up Vancouver Island from where I live. It was like I had found an uncle I didn't know was alive! I got in my car to go and meet the surviving architect of the Orchard Collection. What you have here, then, is an epilogue in the true sense of the word. For me, it is the exclamation point at the end of a ten-year process of studying the collection and writing this book, and it brings the interviews full circle for Stephen fifty years after he and Orchard began to create the collection.

When I first began researching the collection many years ago, I was told that Stephen had died sometime in the 1980s. I'd pictured him as

ABOVE: *Ian Stephen (and Odie) aboard his gillnetter in Nodales Channel, 2004. Photo: Robert Stephen*

being in his fifties, the same age as Orchard, when the two of them were adventuring around the country. However, when I called Stephen to set up our meeting in Campbell River and he mentioned that he was sixteen years Orchard's junior, my whole mental image of him changed. In person, however, he was just as I'd expected: without saying a word, we understood that our shared interest in recording, in British Columbia's history and specifically the Orchard Collection made us instantly familiar to each other. It was not lost on either of us that I was, in my thirties, interviewing this man in his eighties, just as he and Orchard were doing when he was my age—the Orchard Collection had come full circle and now he was the storyteller. As I placed my microphone on the table and set up my recording equipment, his eyes twinkled and we spent the next several hours sitting back, chatting and laughing like old friends.

Ian told me that he was born in Vancouver though his parents lived in Alert Bay. His father, John Clark Stephen, was a wireless operator for local radio, and in 1927 the family moved to Vancouver as his father worked as an assistant radio inspector for two years before moving to Moose Jaw, Saskatchewan. Radio was in the family, and Ian got his first job in 1941 working for CHAB in Moose Jaw as a transmitter operator. Eventually he moved to Vancouver to attend Sprott-Shaw school, where he studied to be a wireless communication technician like his dad (to this day, he still remembers how to send Morse Code), and was then hired as a transmitter operator for the CBC in Winnipeg. Later, while visiting his parents in Vancouver, he was offered a job by Tony Geluch, the chief technician at CBC Vancouver. He moved to the coast with his wife and three children, which is when he first met Orchard.

It had been almost forty-five years since Ian had heard the recordings he made with Orchard. I had brought along some audio tracks from the book, and as he and I sat and listened, I watched him transform from the eighty-five-year-old man before me to the forty-year-old recording engineer, sitting with his headphones on, visiting and recording the old-timers who became his friends. He remembered Paddy Acland and Wiggs O'Neill by name, and told me all about the guy in Victoria who used to be a whaler (Max Lohbrunner). As he listened to Starret recount how Cataline would rub the drink into his hair, Ian laughed and made the motion into his own hair.

"Jeez," he exclaimed, "that brings back memories. Listening to them and realizing that I was there when they were talking, it's just like I am back there with them. It is! It feels like it, especially Starret there. I can see Starret, I can just see him. Oh I wish we'd had video, just to see some of those people again." Thankfully, because of Ian, the exceptional sound quality of the recordings brings to life the voices and the stories they tell. Here, in Ian's own words, are some memories of Imbert Orchard and that time.

· · ·

IAN: He was the greatest guy to work with, but I seen what he was doing and I thought so much of it. Nobody else could work with him. Never had the patience, I guess. This was what Imbert asked me at the start: he said, "Now, do you mind working twelve, fourteen hours a day?" I said, "No. What else am I going to do?" "Well, what about on weekends?" You know, we're away for three weeks. And "Would you rather go home and start again?" I said, "No, we'll do right through." From then on, we just got along perfect. But, boy, that's why once we got working together there was nobody else.

When we were recording these people, he was the one who was sitting there doing that, but I always kept notes and that. And things that I think he'd miss or anything, I was listening to it all the time: if anything happened or something like that, it was up to me to tell him, "Cut it" and we'd straighten it out. I'd stop him lots of times and say, "Okay, the mic's getting off." It was absolutely teamwork.

He treated me as if I was part of what he was doing and he'd, many a time he'd ask, you know, "Should I do this?" "Should I do that?" That made me pretty proud of myself that he was asking that.

ROB: So you'd be listening with headphones on?

IAN: I'd always have headphones, always have headphones. I tried to keep, get out of the room too. I'd get to another room if possible and that way there, you know, it's bad enough for these older people to have a mic around their heads, but they see the equipment go on and me changing tapes and that, so I'd get out of the way.

ROB: To help them forget that they were actually being recorded?

IAN: Yeah, yeah.

ROB: How much of the year would you say you were gone for from about '59 to '66?

IAN: Well, pretty well six months, you know, in the summertime. We never really went out in the winter. We had to go out in the summertime when we could travel, by car and that.

He'd go out for a week, then I'd meet him. You know, leave at Prince Rupert I'd meet him somewhere, fly in. And first thing he did when we met, he'd hand me the keys to the car because that was the understanding. I did the driving. I bet you I drove thousands of miles. That was one thing. The other thing was that, that at night, you know, you may only get six hours' sleep or something like that. I said, "We don't bunk in together. We each get our own room and that's it." That's always the way it went.

But it must have been awful; I know it was hard on my wife. You know, us being on the road. And it must have been also for his wife who, she was a real wonderful person. I tell you, it was one of the best parts of my life was that, with Imbert. You know, we were in our own little world, and one good thing about it, nobody bothered us so much on the CBC. We were on our own. Nobody bothered us. No way.

ROB: The two renegades roaming the countryside.

IAN: Mutt and Jeff. He was tall. I was short. Mutt and Jeff. I'm telling you it, some people would've paid thousands to be in my position to see, you know. There is very little places in B.C. that I haven't been to. All through the Kootenays and all through there up to Queen Charlottes and—. Well, what we could do, we talked to people that built the communities. These were the people that went in, there was nothing there, and listened to their point of view. And each one had a little different history about it. And you have to admire what these people went through, you know, and the tough times they went through. No, it's an experience that you couldn't buy, you couldn't buy. No.

The sweat, you know, that we put in getting those things and where we went: we'd fly in, go in by Indian canoe and horseback. See, we had it figured that we're going out and working, we might as well put every hour we can doing it. We never thought of stopping for supper or this or that. We worked from eight or nine in the morning until ten or eleven at night.

Bella Coola, we were recording right up the valley. In the next motel to us was a couple of anthropologists from the University of B.C. Yeah, and they had come up to get the music and that of this band. And they got on the wrong side of the Chief and them, and they wouldn't have anything to do with them. So one night, I met a couple of Native kids and we got talking. There was only one could say much and, "Do you want to go party?" I said, "Sure." "Okay, come over to our side of town." Very few whites there would go over or would even be invited, so the kids took me over. Boy, they were drinking everything you could think of, you know.

And so I got to meet the Chief. I mentioned to him, "You know, CBC is—" And he says, "I don't like government." And I, "I'm not government, I'm CBC, you know." And talked to him and that and said, "Sure like to get some of your music. We hear you are good." So, right at the end of, I guess around four o'clock, I decided I was going to go back to the motel. So I said to him, "Any chance?" He says, "You be out there on the bank," he says, "in two hours. You be out there, we'll come down."

Sure enough, two hours I got Imbert, shake him, get him up, "We got it, we got something!" We go down, and they come down about a half a dozen of them and played their drums and all that out on the shore of the river. And after, the anthropologists, they heard it, I guess. By the time they got down there, they'd gone and that. They said to me, "How the hell did you ever get that?" I says, "You join 'em, you join 'em." That's all I said to them. And that's what we did with a lot of the people. You go in there and just be one of them and laugh and joke with them and this and that.

It's so much different than just reading about it. But listening to 'em, to get their expression and their feelings, to a lot of them, us having them go back really meant a lot to them too. Because it would bring laughter to them and it would bring tears to them. And some of them when we left, they didn't want us to leave, because they told us all their experiences and that. And it was just like telling the family. And we were family leaving. So there was a lot of times that, you know, recording the people, their expressions you know really came across. I've seen times that we're recording somebody and the first thing you know the three of us are crying because they'd get so emotional and we'd get so emotional. Every time, after you had finished recording maybe—sometimes only maybe a couple of hours, other times two or three days—you almost figured that you were related to 'em because you had the life history. You lived it with them. And, boy, I'm telling you I'd just go home and dream about, you know, being one of these people. Ah Imbert, he put his whole heart into it. He put his whole heart into it.

I'm glad that somebody is going to, to give him credit for what he did. He was a genius. He was the one that could get stuff out of people. I listened to some commentators, you know, on the TV and radio and that. They don't, they can't get out of people what he did. No way. I am glad somebody is taking recognition for what he did.

ROB: Well, for what you both did.

IAN: Well yeah, we both did. We were, we were both very proud of it but I think we both worried that these tapes would disappear and nothing would be done with them. But they didn't realize what we were going through. It's our history, it's really history that couldn't come from better sources, you know. Right from the source. I'm really proud of it and I'm proud that, like you and maybe other people are doing something about it. It's something. It's like it's coming back again, ah it's being reborn. You know, what we did. Wish old Imbert was around.

To listen to this interview as a podcast, visit www.dmpibooks.com or www.memoriestomemoirs.ca

Author's Note

THE OVERWHELMING majority of the 2,090 tapes that hold the 998 interviews in the Orchard Collection were recorded in the field onto 7-inch reels at 7.5 ips [inches per second] in mono by sound technician Ian Stephen between 1959 and 1966. Prior to Orchard's work, the standard method for recording an interview was to place a microphone on a table and record the interviewee from a distance. The recording would inevitably pick up all of the other background noises, and other sounds from the room. Orchard was very committed to changing this method in order to achieve a better sound quality (he was, after all, a radio producer); he wanted to highlight the voice behind the story.

The technicians in the Canadian Broadcasting Corporation's (CBC) workshop developed a new microphone specifically for Orchard, which consisted of a very lightweight wire that hung around the interviewee's neck. This is why Orchard's interviews feature an extremely clear and bright aural quality, particularly for the time. Subsequently, the lapel microphone was invented and is now common for recording voices.

All of the materials contained on the recordings are the property of the CBC; however, the tapes themselves were in Orchard's care. In 1974, after much debate as to where he should keep them, Orchard donated the tapes to the B.C. Archives for preservation and storage. The tapes were stored in a light- and temperature-controlled environment after half-track copies had been made onto 5-inch reels at 3¾ ips. With a complete backup of the entire collection intact, the master tapes were rarely accessed until the summer of 2000.

From 2001 to 2004, Charlene Gregg and I, under the supervision of Allen Specht, worked from the 7-inch original master tapes as we digitized the collection via a direct output from Studer reel-to-reel machines into an HHB 830 series CD burner. All of the recordings in this book are taken directly from clones of the master CDs from those sessions, and I used auto-editing software to edit and in some cases make slight adjustments to the gain before ripping .wav files to the included CDs. What you have here are excerpts from the original field recordings with minimal processing—they are true to the original 1960s recordings. All of the original master tapes, cassette masters, half-track masters, two-track CDs and reference copies are housed at the B.C. Archives; however, the material on the tapes can be accessed by the public through both CBC Archives and the B.C. Archives Web sites.

Acknowledgements

THIS BOOK has been ten years in the making. I owe thanks to a great many people who offered me their faith, support and expertise along the way. First off, back in 2000, David Lemieux recommended me to the staff of the B.C. Archives as an audio preservationist and has continued to offer essential guidance. To J. Robert Davison and Allen Specht for hiring me and allowing me the gift of working on the Orchard Collection, and to all of the staff at the B.C. Archives who, over the years, encouraged and helped me along the way. My heartfelt appreciation to Dennis Duffy, whose expertise on the Orchard Collection is second to none, and to Ember Lundgren, as well as the others on the preservation staff who were always so helpful. Hats off to the knowledgeable staff at the reference desk, and deep appreciation to Kelly-Ann Turkington for promptly assisting me with the photos and answering all my queries.

Knowing that I eventually wanted to produce this book on the Orchard Collection, in 2003 I began work on my MA in History at the University of Victoria. I cannot understate what an empowering experience that was for me; this book is directly linked to my thesis and my time at UVic. Endless respect and gratitude to my colleagues in the master's program, especially Lisa Helps who believed in me from day one, and my professors who pushed me and saw me through: Wendy Wickwire, John Lutz, Georgia Sitara, Richard Mackie, Peter Baskerville, Greg Blue, Tom Saunders and also to Karen Hickton in the grad office. Special thanks to my thesis supervisor, Eric Sager, who helped me wrap my head around the Orchard Collection and with whom I worked so well.

In 2008, Sarah Shugarman introduced me to agent Jan Whitford, who was instrumental in supporting my vision of this project and leading me to Scott McIntyre. My deepest thanks to Scott and the staff at D&M Publishers who have been open to honouring my vision and have trusted in my enthusiasm; and to my editor, Derek Fairbridge, with whom I am always on the same page!

Deep gratitude also to Colin Preston at CBC Archives in Vancouver who has backed this project from the start and given me access and permission to publish this audio collection. The same goes to Gary Mitchell, Director, Collections, Research and Access Services at the Royal B.C. Museum, who actively supported me and saw to it that all of the photos in this book were donated by the Royal B.C. Museum and B.C. Archives. This book really is a testament to the ideal that something extraordinary is possible when everyone puts aside their own agendas to create something bigger than would be possible without the co-operative whole.

Thanks to my brother David Budd who has flown me to many meetings in Vancouver, and to all of my family and friends who continue to be a tremendous support.

Finally, praise to Imbert Orchard and Ian Stephen who travelled British Columbia on a very limited budget and accumulated this unbelievable collection for us all to learn from and enjoy.

A Note on Sources

MOST OF the material in this book was gathered from listening to the interviewees themselves, and other interviewees from the Orchard Collection. The majority of the contextual information was gathered at the Provincial Archives of British Columbia and numerous city archives and Web sites. For other background information, I relied on the wonderful scholarship of several B.C. historians, including Jean Barman's *The West Beyond the West* (Toronto: University of Toronto Press, 1991), Robin Fisher's *Contact and Conflict* (Vancouver: UBC Press, 1992) and *Old Bill Miner* (Surrey: Heritage House, 2001). I also consulted several censuses for demographic details. This work was also influenced by several oral theorists and historians, including Julie Cruikshank, Renato Rosaldo, Alessandro Portelli, John Tosh, Cole Harris, Ian McKay, Paul Thompson, Alan Lomax and many others. Finally, Dennis Duffy at the B.C. Archives was a remarkable source of information about the Orchard Collection and Orchard himself.